DATE DUE

DE 15 '02			
NY 27 '03			
FE 10 '05			
AP 1 '08			
DE 19 '08			

DEMCO 38-296

HEALTH CARE SYSTEMS IN JAPAN AND THE UNITED STATES:

A Simulation Study and Policy Analysis

Research Monographs in Japan-U.S. Business & Economics

series editors
Rama V. Ramachandran
Ryuzo Sato
Stern School of Business
New York University

Other books published in the series:

Sato, Ryuzo/Ramachandran, Rama
  Conservation Laws and Symmetry: Applications to Economics and Finance

Sato, Ramachandran, and Hori
  Organization, Performance, and Equity: Perspectives on the Japanese Economy

HEALTH CARE SYSTEMS IN JAPAN AND THE UNITED STATES:
A Simulation Study and Policy Analysis

Ryuzo Sato
New York University

Elias Grivoyannis
University of North Carolina
at Greensboro

Barbara Byrne
New York University

Chengping Lian
Shanghai Institute of Economic Development

The Center for Japan-U.S. Business and Economic Studies
Leonard N. Stern School of Business
New York University

Kluwer Academic Publishers
Boston/Dordrecht/London

Norwell, Massachusetts 02061 USA

Distributors for all other countries:
Kluwer Academic Publishers Group
Distribution Centre
Post Office Box 322
3300 AH Dordrecht, THE NETHERLANDS

Library of Congress Cataloging-in-Publication Data

Health care systems in Japan and the United States : a simulation
   study and policy analysis / Ryuzo Sato . . . [et al.].
      p.   cm.   -- (Research monographs in Japan-U.S. business &
   economics)
      Includes bibliographical references and index.
      ISBN 0-7923-9948-X
      1. Medical care--Japan--Finance.   2. Medical policy--Japan.
   3. Medical care--United States--Finance.   4. Medical policy--United
   States.   I. Satō, Ryūzō, 1931-   II. Series.
   RA410.55.J3H443   1997
   338.4'33621'0952--dc21   97-21873
                                                          CIP

Copyright © 1997 by Kluwer Academic Publishers

Printed on acid-free paper.

Printed in the United States of America

CONTENTS

PREFACE

The health care sector has become a major component of the contemporary economies of Japan and the United States. It absorbs significant proportions of the GDP in both countries and places increasing stress on private, government and corporate budgets. As their income rises, the citizens of Japan and the United States choose to allocate increasing portions of it on health care services because of the direct contribution of health care services to prolonged life expectancy, reduced morbidity, or other indicators of improved health and well-being. The health care sector is a major source of employment and affects the lives of all citizens. Adequate health care services are expected to have an important contribution to the quality of human life in any society. With so much at stake, arrangements for planning, financing, and operating health care service systems have increasingly come to be regarded as important economic and political issues.

The political importance of health care is evidenced by the health care reform proposals of the Clinton administration in the United States and the deep involvement of the government in the medical care security system in Japan. As policymakers in both countries look ahead to the coming decades, they realize that the imperatives of economic restructuring, globalization, and their rapidly aging societies will affect the way in which health care is organized, delivered, and financed. These expected changes provide both opportunities and challenges for the policymakers of both countries. Financing the health care needs of their aging populations and reassigning priorities to various other domestic and international issues and problems on their national agenda, are basic constraints over which policymakers show a great concern. In response to these challenges, different avenues have been explored in an attempt to identify optimal policy recommendations.

Health policymakers in Japan, for example, have been urged to exploit the "vitality of the private sector" (*minkan katsuryoku* or *minkatsu* for short) in adjusting the medical care security system to meet the needs and priorities of the future. One response to *minkatsu* has been the opening of the health insurance market to both domestic and foreign private insurance services. In the United States, the Clinton administration is proposing a universal health insurance plan as the foundation of its health care reforms for the future. Much of the ongoing debate of the Clinton proposals is around issues of cost containment and the allocation of health care services, the labor market effect of financing universal coverage, the redistribution effects of the proposed health care reforms (community rating versus experience rating practices), how universal coverage should be financed, whether costs should be controlled through incentives or budgets, who should bear the risk of reform, etc.

Most of the policy recommendations in the health care financing debate take a micro-management approach. Our monograph takes a very different route. It takes a macroeconomic policy outlook. Most of the current literature identifies the increasing trend of national expenditures on health care services as an alarming problem for the aging societies of the future and try to deal with the problem by identifying ways of reducing, or controlling, the rate of growth of health care expenditures. Our monograph deals with the fundamental question of whether or not the anticipated increasing rate of growth in health care expenditures of the future could be financially absorbed by society's increasing income and output. We consider alternative scenarios of productivity rates of growth for the non-health care sectors of the Japanese and the U.S. economies and simulate the absorption process under which increasing incomes manage to finance (absorb) increasing health care expenditures.

In our approach, we assess the magnitude and significance of the problem, before trying to solve it. This step is very important for the following obvious reason. If attainable rates of productivity growth in the non-health care sectors of the two economies could absorb the future growth rates of health care expenditures, then the problem of financing these expenditures in the future is automatically solved. If this is the case, then, the micro-management approaches adopted by other researchers should focus on operational issues of increasing efficiency rather than containing costs through budgets and price controls or administrative rationing in the delivery of health care services.

This monograph addresses not only *if* but also *how* health care financing could in the future be ethically, safely, and economically accomplished. It identifies the right questions that must be answered and the balance that must be sought among the dilemmas and paradoxes raised by the realities of financing health care services in the future. It identifies the magnitude of constrained resources for payers in the rate of growth of their labor productivity, and eliminates the pressure of proposed health care reforms which present an array of unknowns for health care providers. In addition, it provides hope for policymakers who are concerned about the anticipated demographic changes which are expected to impose unprecedented demands for care of the frail elderly and persons with special needs, chronic diseases and chronically acute conditions.

We wish to thank Kathleen Lowy and Robin Romeo for their word processing work.

Ryuzo Sato
Elias Grivayannis
Barbara Byrne
Chengping Lian

CHAPTER 1

OVERVIEW

The extrapolated growth of the health care sector in both the United States and Japan is of concern to the specialist and laymen alike. Both economies have witnessed very rapid growth in health care services, with a greater share of labor and capital being absorbed by that sector in the two economies. The trade-off between invest-ment in resources associated with life extension vs. that associated with the en-hancement of the productivity of the workforce is of vital importance to both Japan and the United States as both countries have witnessed unprecedented growth in their respective aged populations. The trend of a rapidly expanding elderly class will continue well in the 21st century, as will rising medical expenditures that are required to care for this elderly class. Just how the two economies can sustain this growth in health care spending, as health care must be financed by resources from the more productive sectors, is the concern of this study.

To some extent health care serves are an intermediary good to production. That is, medical services maintain the health of the workforce which sustains the produc-tivity of this working population, but only up to a certain level. Sick workers who receive health care recover faster and their recovery increases their productivity. When health care expenditures enhance society's ability to provide consumer bene-fits in the future, they could be considered an investment. Using health care beyond a certain level, shifts it from an investment good into a consumption good. Beyond a certain level of health care utilization, the labor productivity per unit of health care utilization starts declining. When utilization of health care services has no impact on labor productivity it would conceivably be considered a consumer's good. Health care also becomes a consumption good when used by the non-working population, the aged and the disabled. When the utilization of health care services is a con-sumption good, the funds to pay for it will have to come either from the lifetime savings accumulation of the health care recipients, from the lifetime income of the health care providers, or from the government budget. Consumption of health care by the aged has two important policy implications: finding the funds to pay for it, and justifying the required resource allocation choice. When utilization of health care services is an investment good, the resulting higher labor productivity would justify the funds to pay for it. In the case of the elderly, however, such policy questions as how much and how often are generally addressed within partisan circles of policy debate (as recent history has shown). The controversies surrounding discussion of health financing will absorb more and more of the energies of both the U.S. and Japan's societies over the next decade or more.

1.1 Decomposition of Health Care Expenditures

Spending more money on health care services as a percentage of the Gross Domestic Product (GDP) cannot in itself reveal if a nation is getting better-off or worse-off over time. To answer this question we should look at three components of the change in health care expenditures: price changes, utilization of health care changes and population changes.

Let $H = 1 +$ [annual percentage increase in health-care spending]

$HP = 1 +$ [annual percentage increase in health-care prices]

$V = 1 +$ annual percentage increase in volume-intensity, and

$POP = 1 +$ annual percentage increase in population

Then we arrive at the following identity in health economics:

$H = HP * V * POP$

Table 1 provides numerical values for this identity for a number of industrialized countries including the United States and Japan. It indicates that for Japan the annual compound rate of growth of nominal health care expenditures between 1975 and 1987 was 9.1 percent as a result of a 4.1 percent annual compound increase in health care prices, a 4.0 percent annual compound increase in per capita volume-intensity, and a 0.8 percent annual compound increase in population.

For the United States the annual compound rate of growth of nominal health care expenditures during the same period was 11.7 percent as a result of an 8.1 percent annual compound increase in health care prices, a 2.3 percent annual compound increase in per capita volume-intensity, and a 1.0 percent annual compound increase in population. These figures suggest that in both the United States and Japan, people

TABLE 1

Decomposition of health expenditure increases into price, population, and volume increase:
Selected countries, 1975 - 87 Annual Compound rate of growth, 1975 - 1987

Country	Share of health expenditure to GDP 1975	Nominal health ex- penditure growth	Health care price deflator	Real health expenditure growth	Population growth	Per capita volume- intensity growth	Share of health ex- penditure to GDP 1987
Canada	7.3	11.8	8.6	2.9	1.0	1.9	8.6
France	6.8	13.4	7.6	5.4	0.5	4.9	8.6
Germany	7.8	6.2	3.9	2.2	-0.1	2.3	8.2
Italy	5.8	17.6	14.9	2.3	0.3	2.0	6.9
United Kingdom	5.5	13.0	10.8	2.0	0.1	1.9	6.1
U.S.A.	8.4	11.7	8.1	3.3	1.0	2.3	11.2
Japan	5.5	9.1	4.1	4.8	0.8	4.0	6.8
Mean	6.7	11.8	8.3	3.3	0.5	2.8	8.1

Source: Organization for Economic Cooperation and Development: Health Data File, 1989.

are spending more on health care services year after year mainly because of health care price inflation and secondly because of the increase in the pre capita utilization of health care services. Population growth in both countries contributes an insignificant amount in the growth rate of health care expenditures.[1]

1.2 Related Literature

Economists have analyzed the competition among users of resources within an overlapping generations framework.[2] By allowing the population of retirees to fluctuate, overlapping generation models have been used to explain cycles in per capita income that are motivated by endogenous fluctuations in the demand for health. This is done by including the effects of *health capital* on mortality and the supply of labor in efficiency units. The mortality aspect of health capital was included in the seminal literature on health (Grossman, 1972) and was later extended by Ehrlich and Chuma (1990).

The aging of a population may not only be due to the influence of exogenous demographic, biological or technological factors but also to systematic variations in individuals' demand for longevity. Grossman (1972) and Ehrlich and Chuma (1990) treat longevity as an endogenous factor on the assumption that some technologies exist through which it is possible to convert basic economic resources into marginal increments in opportunities for longer life. In Grossman's work the choice of longevity is viewed as an indirect outcome of the choice of "health capital", to be produced through investments in health augmentation or maintenance. Thus, in an intertemporal setting, the effective life horizon of individuals becomes a choice variable like any other "private" good. Extending Grossman's work, Ehrlich and Chuma (1990) derive the demand for health in conjunction with that for longevity and related consumption choices, assuming that investment in health is subject to increasing costs, and health production is subject to diminishing returns.

Through such models economists managed to analyze the dynamics of collective aging and explain the *paternalistic* role of the medical community in the service of the elderly.

1.3 Objective of this Study

In our analysis, we use a contemporaneous generations model and treat society's investment in life extension and maintenance for the elderly as a substitute to the future productivity of youth. The main contribution of our approach is the following: We can show that the price instability in the health care sector is a result of the manner in which costs and prices relate to labor productivity. By utilizing a mixture of empirically derived data and realistic assumptions regarding demographic and productivity growth trends, we simulate sets of alternative scenarios for Japan and the United States and describe the necessary conditions for financing the rising health care needs of the aging societies in the two countries.

Under realistic conditions, the simulations show that the expanding health care expenditures can be accommodated by the two economic systems if they can maintain their current rates of productivity growth. What the aging societies of Japan and the United States need in the future are sustainable rates of productivity growth, especially in their respective non-health sectors. The higher productivity growth rates in the non-health sectors will help to absorb the higher health care costs. Also, a more rapid rate of productivity growth in the health care sector itself via mechanization may increase efficiency and thereby mitigate high health care costs. However, this would not be consistent with quality improvement in health care because more mechanization would tend to reduce human interaction.

1.4 Organization of the Monograph

This monograph is divided into two parts. Chapters 2 through 5, are descriptive in nature. Chapter 2 takes a look at demographic changes over the last fifty years that have dramatically increased the life expectancy of Japanese and American citizens. We focus particularly on the rising ratio of elderly and the impact this has had on the allocation of health care services in the two countries. Chapter 3 provides a detail profile of health care utilization of the elderly and Chapter 4 details the paternalistic manner in which health care services are provided to the elderly in both countries thereby reducing the effectiveness of market allocation of health care services. Chapter 5 details the expenditure and financing trends of health care in the two countries.

Chapters 6 through 9 deal with our model and simulation results. A more detailed discussion of our approach is presented in Chapter 6. The simulation model and its various parameters are discussed in Chapter 7. (A mathematical specification of the model is presented in Appendix I.) Our simulation results for Japan and the United States over the time horizon from 1990 to 2025 are discussed in Chapters 8 and 9. Concluding remarks are contained in Chapter 10.

Notes

[1] For a more extensive discussion on this decomposition see: OECD, Social Policy Studies, No. 7, Health Care Systems in Transition: The Search for Efficiency, Paris, France, 1990.
[2] Starting with Samuelson, 1958; Diamond, 1965; Farmer, 1986; Reichlin, 1986, and most recently, Ehrlich and Lui, 1991.

CHAPTER 2

DEMOGRAPHIC CHANGES IN
JAPAN AND THE UNITED STATES

At the same time the United States and Japanese societies have grown richer, they have also grown older. One of the most pervasive trends in the United States and Japan is the overall aging of their population. The proportion of the United States population aged 65 or over has grown slowly but steadily from 8.1 percent in 1950 to 11.3 percent in 1980, it became nearly 13 percent in 1990 and is expected to reach 22.9 percent by 2050. For Japan the figures are 4.9 percent in 1950, 9.1 percent in 1980, 11.9 percent in 1990, and 23.5 percent by 2050 (see Table 2). The significant implication from an aging society in the U.S. and Japan is based on the underlying repercussions of aging: As one gets older and their life expectancy increases, their health deteriorates faster and they use more medical care services.

2.1 Decreasing Fertility Rates

One reason for this demographic trend is the change in the fertility rate of the U.S. and Japanese populations. Japan's fertility rate fell sharply from 4.5 in 1947 (the postwar baby boom) to 2.1 in the 1960s, and to 1.5 in 1993. In the case of the United States the fertility rate fell from 2.93 in 1965 to 1.77 in 1975 and to 1.87 in 1987. The "baby boomers" who were born in the late 1940's will be over 65 years old by the year 2010, and will be replaced in the labor force by the smaller number of the babies that were born in the 1970's and 1980's.

This drop in the fertility rate is partly a result of the postwar migration of the population from rural to urban areas that is commonly associated with an occupational shift from the agricultural to manufacturing sector.

TABLE 2

AGE DISTRIBUTION OF THE U.S. AND JAPAN POPULATION

Year	Percent Over 65 Years Old in the U.S.A.	Percent over 65 Years Old in Japan
1950	8.1%	4.9%
1955	8.7%	5.3%
1960	9.2%	5.7%
1965	9.5%	6.3%
1970	9.8%	7.1%
1975	10.5%	7.9%
1980	11.3%	9.1%
1985	11.9%	10.3%
1990	12.6%	11.9%
2000	13.0%	16.3%
2010	13.9%	20.0%
2015	15.8%	22.5%
2020	17.7%	23.6%
2025	17.9%	23.4%
2050	22.9%	23.5%

Source: U.S. Department of Commerce, Bureau of the Census, "Current Population Reports: Population Estimates and Projections, Series P-25, No. 1018." Japan: Ministry of Health and Welfare, Annual Report, November 1990, Table I-1-2.

TABLE 3

FERTILITY RATE: AVERAGE BIRTHS PER WOMAN OF
CHILDBEARING AGE FOR
THE UNITED STATES AND JAPAN

Country	Year 1965	Year 1970	Year 1975	Year 1980	Year 1985	Year 1991
U.S.A.	2.93	2.48	1.77	1.84	1.84	1.80
Japan	2.14	2.13	1.19	1.75	1.76	1.53

Sources: "Demographic Yearbook", United Nations; "Recent Demographic Developments in the Member States of the Council of Europe"; the central statistics bureaus of each country.

TABLE 4

PERCENTAGE OF JAPANESE HOUSEHOLDS LIVING IN CITIES
VS. RURAL AREAS

Percent Living	Year 1955	Year 1960	Year 1965	Year 1970	Year 1975	Year 1980	Year 1985
In Cities	59.0	66.5	71.0	75.0	78.6	79.2	79.7
In Rural Areas	41.0	33.5	29.0	25.0	21.4	20.8	20.3

Source: "National Census", Statistics Bureau, General Affairs Agency.

Table 4 indicates, almost 80 percent of the Japanese families were urban dwellers in 1985. Many of these urban dwellers are double-income families where both husband and wife are going out to work. For parents working in the agricultural sector their children were perceived as an asset because they supplied labor. For parents working in the cities their children were perceived as a liability because they have to pay childcare while at work. As a result of a decreasing rural population and an increasing urban population the average number of children per family declined both in the United States and Japan. This decline in the birth rate decreases the forthcoming working population and at the same time increases the percentage of elderly in the overall population.

TABLE 5

PERCENTAGE OF UNMARRIED WOMEN AGED 20-24
IN THE UNITED STATES AND JAPAN

Country	Year 1950	Year 1960	Year 1970	Year 1980
U.S.A.	32.3%	28.4%	36.3%	51.3%
Japan	55.2%	68.3%	71.7%	77.7%

Source: "Demographic Yearbook", United Nations.

The second factor for the fertility decline was the later average age for women's first marriages since the early 1970s. This age is now 26 years for Japan, the second highest in the world after Sweden.[3] Many women, both in the U.S. and Japan delay their marriages because of their increasing utility from higher education and career opportunities. Female participation in the work force in Japan increased three-fold over a thirty year period numbering 5.1 million in 1955 to 15.9 million in 1985. Women in the workforce tend to delay childbearing or choose to forego having children altogether. Fewer women having children translates into a lower average number of children per family.

The progress towards later marriage can also be looked at in terms of the increase in ratios of younger people who are not married. In 1982, the Institute of Population Problems in Japan carried out its eighth National Fertility Survey. To the question whether people as yet unmarried wished to be so, 2.3 percent of men and 4.1 percent of women responded that they "do not plan to marry during their lifetimes." In 1987 (five years later), during the ninth National Fertility Survey these rates increased to 4.5 percent for men and 4.6 percent for women. Fewer women marrying yields a lower fertility rate for the overall population.

2.2 Increasing Life Expectancy

One factor that is an indication of "development" is the decline in the mortality rate. Japan has the highest life expectancy of all major industrial countries. Average life-expectancy for males has increased from 50.1 years in 1947 to 76.3 years in 1993 and for females from 54 years to 82.5 years during the same period.[4] Initially, increased life expectancy was due to a sharp fall in the mortality rate among children under one year old thanks to improvements in nutrition and sanitary conditions. Better health care for the elderly has also significantly increased life expectancy at retirement age and beyond by delaying the approach of death, since death is no longer so imminent once one's "health capital" drops to a critically minimum level. In Japan, average life expected (years remaining at age 65) for males and females were 16.4 and 20.6 in 1993 respectively.

A significant cause for the growing share of the elderly in the total population in both the U.S. and Japan has to do with the modern technological advances that our economies have had. A rapid rise in Japanese and U.S. per capita GDP and income in the postwar period, brought on by major industrial technological advances have created spillovers for the medical profession in the form of better medical procedures. In addition, a more *equitable* distribution of both income and medical services in both countries, especially since the middle 1960s in the United States and the early 1970s in Japan, has also contributed better access to health services. As a result, medical standards for all citizens have risen substantially in both countries.

Greater access to better medical care has increased the utilization of health care

Greater access to better medical care has increased the utilization of health care services by the aging population. The demand for "health capital," defined as the equipment used by the medical profession, has grown due to the rapidly deteriorating average health of an ever older elderly class. This stock can be maintained or augmented through investments in medical technology. Yet, paradoxically, increasing investments leads to improved health and, as a result, longer lives. How to address this paradox is beyond the scope of this monograph.

2.3 Dependency Ratio

While the lower fertility rate and longer life expectancy yield a higher percentage of people over 65 years in the entire population, over time, the over-all dependence rate of the non-working population on the labor force has remained relatively constant in the United States. The population dependency ratio is the ratio of 16 years and younger and 65 years and older to the entire population. The lower fertility rates both reduce the percentage of those that are 16 years and younger and increase the percentage of those that are 65 years and older. Likewise, the labor force as a percentage of the entire population has not changed significantly, since most baby boomers have been in the labor force since the mid-sixties and are not due to retire until 2010. The consistency of the population dependency ratio to the labor force suggests that the U.S. is able to support the *dependent* segment of its population, but the shift in this *dependent* segment toward more elderly contradicts this premise. Current data on health care utilization rates shows that not only has the U.S. economy shifted away from productive industries concentrated in manufacturing towards services, but that the *service-producing* industry with the highest share of growth is, in fact, health services. As of July, 1995, 9.3 million are employed in health services, which represents a growth of 265,000 or 3 percent over July 1994. The health care industry employs 8 percent of the nations labor force. Of these, 1.5 million in Doctors Offices, 1.7 million in Nursing care facilities, 3.8 million in hospitals and 600,00 in home health care services.

In the next few decades, both the U.S. and Japan will be experiencing an increasing number of elderly, (as shown in Table 2) for the reasons discussed above: the aging of the "baby boomers" generation coupled with flat growth in the fertility rate; and an increasing number of elders who live longer than before because of the rising life expectancy in the population of the two countries over time.

2.4 Per Capita Utilization of Health Care Services

The annual compound increase in per capita utilization of health care services was 4 percent for Japan and 2.30 percent for the 1975 to 1987 period (Table 1). This increase in per capita volume intensity was a result of economic growth and higher national income, but also a result of demographic changes.

The U.S. economy has grown steadily since World War II at an average annual rate of about 1.75 percent in real purchasing power, while the Japanese economy has been growing even faster.[5] With economic growth, personal income increases and the propensity to buy more and different things also increases. Those with higher income have better health insurance than those with lower income and this leads them to use more medical care than before. The income elasticity of medical services estimates[6] (Table 6) suggest that for every 10 percent increase in nominal per capita GDP, the nominal per capita expenditure on health care services will increase by 13 percent in the United States and Japan, by 12 percent in France and by 11 percent in the United Kingdom and Germany. This indicates that health care services qualifies as a luxury good in our industrialized societies.[7] As income in our societies increases (say by 10 percent) we decide to spend proportionally more money out of our income (approximately 13 percent of it) on health care services.

TABLE 6

**ELASTICITY OF PER CAPITA HEALTH CARE EXPENDITURE
RELATIVE TO PER CAPITA GROSS DOMESTIC PRODUCT
(GDP), 1975-1987**

Country	Elasticity	
	Nominal	Real
France	1.2	3.1
Germany	1.1	0.9
Japan	1.3	1.4
United Kingdom	1.1	1.0
U.S.A.	1.3	1.1

Source: Organization for Economic Cooperation and Development Health Care Systems in Transition, Paris 1990.

Such patterns of income spending change the composition of national output over time and result in a growing share of health care services in GDP. In 1960, the share of health care services in GDP was 5.2 percent for the U.S. and 2.9 percent for Japan. Thirty years later, it more than doubled for both countries. In 1990, the share of health care services in GDP was 12 percent for the United States and 6.8 percent for Japan.

Notes

[3] Yashiro, 1995

[4] Yashiro, 1995

[5] The Japanese economy has grown at an average annual rate of 10 percent from 1945 to 1970 and 4 to 5 percent thereafter until 1990. The growth rate dropped down to 3.6 percent in 1991; 0.3 percent in 1992; -0.2 percent in 1993, and 0.7 percent in 1994. The Japanese government forecast of economic growth for fiscal 1995 is 2.8 percent, while that of private research institutes is only 1.8 percent for the same period.

[6] See George J. Scheiber and Jean-Pierre Poullier, "Overview of International Comparisons of Health Care Expenditures" in OECD, Social Policy Studies, NO. 7, "Health Care Systems in Transition: The Search for Efficiency", OECD, Paris, France, 1990, p. 11. Income Elasticity estimates based on time series should be interpreted carefully. An income elasticity calculation presumes that the same choice set of health care services was available at varying income levels. When the time series are very long the choice set may be significantly different because of technical progress and in such a case the elasticity estimate is subject to some speculation.

[7] For an interesting discussion on this issue see: Parkin, David, Alistair McGuire, and Biran Yule, "Aggregate Health Care Expenditures and National Income: Is Health Care a Luxury Good?", Journal of Health Economics 6, 1987, pp. 109-128.

CHAPTER 3

HEALTH CARE SERVICES UTILIZATION
PROFILES AMONG THE ELDERLY

Because the absolute and relative numbers of older adults have been and are expected to continue increasing, the disproportional consumption of health care resources by the elderly has stimulated a considerable amount of research on the
health and health services utilization of older adults.[8]

According to a previous review of the literature by Mossey, Havens, and Wolinsky (1989), the three most important findings from these studies were that: (a) most
older adults are consistent users of health services, although this is more so for physicians than hospital utilization; (b) a small proportion of older adults consistently
make extensive use of both physician and hospital services; and (c) need is the most
prominent indicator of the volume of health services utilization among consistent
users.

By the year 2040, the baby boomers of the U.S. and Japan will reach their eight-
ies and nineties. The underlying biological repercussion of aging mentioned above
addressed the increasing propensity of consumption on medical care as one ages and
their health stock deteriorates faster.[9] The rate of hospital days per 1,000 persons
aged 85+ is more than two times that of men and women 65-74 years.[10] The rate of
nursing home residents per 1,000 is 13 times higher for men 85+ than for men 65-74
years, and 18 times higher for women 85+ than for women 65-74 years. Estimates[11]
of the over-65 population expected to have a long-term disability in the year 2040
range from 14.8 to 22.6 million people, compared to approximately 5.1 million older
people experiencing a long-term disability in 1986 (an increase ranging from 190
percent to 343 percent). It appears that the economic growth along with the aging of
our societies will be accompanied by a growing need for per capita utilization of
health care services in the years to come.

TABLE 7

RATES OF USE OF SELECTED HEALTH SERVICES PER
1,000 PEOPLE IN THE U.S. BY AGE AND GENDER

Gender and Age	Physician Contacts (per 1,000)	Hospital Days of Care (per 1,000)	Nursing Home Residents (per 1,000)
Male			
65-74	8,113.0	2,445.2	10.8
75-84	8,667.9	4,263.7	43.0
85 +	11,411.6	5,371.4	145.7
total 65 +	8,472.7		
Female			
65-74	8,599.2	2,174.3	13.8
75-84	9,652.6	3,531.8	66.4
85 +	11,497.2	4,915.1	250.1
total 65 +	9,197.6	2,938.6	57.9

Source: K. F. Ferraro and T.T.H. Wan, "Health Needs and Services for Older Adults:
Evaluating Policies for an Aging Society". p. 239 in S.M. Stahl, (ed.) The Legacy
of Longevity: Health and Health Care in Late Life, Newbury Park, Sage Publications, 1990, pp. 235-269.

Although older Americans represent just one-eighth of the population, they account for more than one-third of the total health care expenditures (Department of
Health and Human Services, 1990). The use of health services by older adults, however, is not homogeneous. Among non-institutionalized older adults, less than one-
eighth account for over seven-tenths of that group's health care expenditures.[12]
Thus, disproportional health services utilization has been documented for older
adults both as a class[13] and as a subgroup of individuals.[14]

3.1   A Behavior Model of Health Care Services Among the Elderly

The most frequently used approach in analyzing and predicting utilization health
care services among the elderly has been the behavioral model of Andersen.[15] The
behavioral model identifies predisposing, enabling, and need factors as the primary
determinants of health care service use. Predisposing factors are exogenous variables in this model and are seen as creating a propensity toward use by the elderly
and their family members. These variables are not seen as causing service use di-

rectly, but rather are included to reflect the fact that some families have a greater propensity toward health care service use than others. Predisposing factors include social structural variables such as age, sex, marital status, race, and family composition, as well as attitudes such as health beliefs. Enabling factors reflect the fact that even though the elderly and their families may be predisposed to use health care services, certain conditions must be met to *enable* families to attain them. As conceptualized by Andersen (1968), enabling conditions include two components: family resources and community resources., Finally, even assuming a predisposition to use health care services and the ability to do so, the elderly and their families must see a need for a particular service. Need, viewed in the behavioral model as the most proximal cause of service use, is assessed according to the extent of illness as perceived by the elderly and their family members. In other words, need for a service depends upon who is defining that need.

Andersen (1968) further characterizes health care services as either discretionary or nondiscretionary. The elderly and their families are assumed to exert less discretion in the use of certain health care services because access to such services is usually regulated by providers or other professionals. For example, hospitalization would involve less discretion than deciding whether to use adult day care because a physician makes the decision to admit the patient into the hospital. The behavioral model assumes that the more discretionary the service, the more important will be the predisposing and enabling factors in explaining service use. Use of discretionary services is more likely to be a function of family characteristics, values, or resources. For less discretionary services, need factors will be most important. Most of the health care utilization by elderly is covered by now-pervasive entitlement or health insurance programs, thereby reducing the importance of predisposing and enabling factors in the decision to use services.

Andersen (1968) viewed all decisions regarding the use of health services as family decisions where family "caregivers" play an important role. In care giving situations, which are characterized by dependency of the elder on the family member, need is likely to be defined jointly by the caregiver and the elder. In such circumstances, the decision to use services is likely to be made by considering the joint needs of both the dependent elder and the caregiver. As a result, the nature of the caregiving relationship-a predisposing factor-interacts with perceptions of need to influence service use. Focusing on both the patient and caregiver rather than the individual seems appropriate for several reasons. First, because the caregiver is actively involved in the provision of care, need characteristics of the caregiver (e.g., caregiver's health) also affect in-home service use by elders.[16] Second, caregivers perform referral and gatekeeping functions in the elder's knowledge about and use of formal services. Third, cultural influences on the expectations for care by the caregiver and elder exist within the family and are likely to influence perceptions of need.[17]

A caregiver who is the spouse of the elder may be more likely to perceive outside assistance as unnecessary than would the adult-child of the elder who is trying to maintain a job, a separate household, and so on. Such interactions between predispositions to use services and need factors can be expected to affect primarily the use of discretionary services (i.e., services under the control of the family). Nondiscretionary health care services, use of which is generally dictated by providers, should continue to be explained primarily by need characteristics.[18]

3.2 The Impact of Need Factors in Services Utilization

Changes in health is of particular concern to older adults because good health is closely related to general well-being.[19] Health among older adults is complicated by the interaction of diseases that accompany the aging process.[20] Indeed, chronic illness, and mortality contribute significantly to increased psychological distress among many older adults. For example, patients with chronic obstructive pulmonary disease (COPD) typify chronic illness in old age.[21] Decreases in lung elasticity and functional capacity, common to the aging process,[22] are exacerbated by COPD. COPD patients typically experience a prolonged course of illness marked by chronic shortness of breath and coughing and require an extended period of medical care. COPD patients endure a progressive deterioration of physical functioning. In addition to their significant physical impairment, patients with COPD have been found to exhibit psychological distress[23] as well as impaired cognitive functioning.[24]

Health in old age also deteriorates because of significant dysphoria[25] attributed to the significant lifestyle changes that confront older adults[26] including the deaths of loved ones, changes in social roles, and impaired health.

3.2.1 Poor Vision and its Complementary Health Care Problems for the Elderly

Poor vision adds a risk factor for the elderly, in that it leads to falling (Over, 1966; Verms, 1991), which claimed 2.2 million victims in 1985 in the United States[27] and an estimated 9.8 billion dollars in cost.[28] The human eye experiences progressive functional decline with age.[29] The incidence of cataracts, which are an opaque layer of film that grows over one's eyes, rises as one ages. Poor vision can contribute to a fall directly through inaccurate perception of the environment, as well as indirectly through difficulty in coordinating balance.[30] For hip fractures, both visual disability, such as recognizing a friend across the room[31] and impaired visual acuity[32] have been shown to be risk factors. Impaired visual acuity was also shown to be a risk factor for serious injurious falls (i.e., fractures, dislocations, or lacerations requiring stitches.[33] Moreover, visual-perception disorders may be related to cognition, as has been shown with dementia.[34]

3.2.2 Dental Care for the Elderly

Approximately $34 billion were spent on dental services in 1990; this compares to $53 billion for nursing home care and $126 billion of physician services.[35] The past three decades have been characterized by higher percentages of persons who reported having been to a dentist within the previous year.[36] This increase has been especially true for older adults whose use percentage has more than doubled since 1957. Although a consensus does not exist regarding an appropriate interval for dental attendance, there is general agreement among clinicians that persons at high risk for dental decay and/or periodontal diseases need to be observed more frequently than on an annual basis. Edentulous persons, or those with no teeth, need constant observation for oropharyngeal cancer screening, detection of noncancerous oral lesions, and follow-up care of prostheses.

3.2.3 The Grown Pain of the Grown Old

Because of the increased incidence of chronic diseases, falls, and other health problems associated with aging, the elderly are at greater risk for experiencing both acute and chronic pain. Roy and Thomas (1986) conducted a survey to determine the prevalence of chronic pain problems among the elderly. Eighty-three percent of the subjects reported pain. Of those, 88 percent attributed their pain to musculoskeletal disorders resulting in back, joint, and muscle pain. Only 7 percent reported that their pain was of recent onset and of short duration. The remaining subjects reported having pain problems for more than 1 year, confirming that pain in the elderly is often chronic. Pain treatment was also assessed. The majority of patients (84 percent) were receiving or using analgesics to treat their pain. Seventy-four percent of the subjects with pain reported that it interfered with activities of daily living.

In a related study to describe the scope of the problem of pain for the elderly in a long-term care facility conducted by Ferrell, Ferrell and Osterweil (1990), 71 percent of the subjects indicated the presence of pain at least some of the time; 66 percent of these subjects indicate intermittent pain, and 34 percent indicate constant pain. Major sources of pain were low back pain (40 percent), arthritis of appendicular joints (24 percent), previous fracture sites (14 percent), and neuropathies (11 percent). Substantial effects of pain on function were reported by 77 percent of the subjects.

Pain not only troubles the elderly more often than any other type of symptom, but is also associated with activity disturbances, including walking, household activities and chores, sleep, and social and leisure activities more than other reported symptoms. The higher prevalence of joint pain is not unexpected given the incidence of osteoarthritis and connective tissue disorders affecting the elderly (Kart, Metress, and Metress, 1988). The relatively high prevalence of high leg pain is also not surprising and often occurs in the elderly with arthritis, varicose veins, and following excessive muscle activity.[37]

Pain is a multidimensional phenomenon, and can be experienced in many different forms. Important dimensions of pain include frequency, severity, chronicity, and the level of interference with activities. The persistence of pain with advancing age is a typical warning sign of illness or pathology and plays an important role in perceptions of health status. Persistence of pain among the elderly results in their increasing hospitalization and institutionalization. A study by Bucquet and Curtis (1986) indicated that "physical symptoms of pain" was one of four characteristics significantly associated with physician consultation (along with emotions, isolation, and immobility). Respondents reporting pain or physical immobility were almost twice as likely to have consulted their physician in the past 2 weeks as those not reporting these symptoms. Chronic pain results in more frequent and extended use of health services.

3.2.4 Decline in Physical Activity by the Elderly and its Risks to their Health

The benefits of exercise in improving cardiovascular risk factors and measured fitness status are well documented.[38] Exercise by older adults improves their cardiovascular fitness[39], increases muscle strength, bone density, and lowers blood pressure.[40]

A 1985 National Health Interview Survey (NHIS) found that activity levels decline with age.[41] Although many elders understand the importance of physical activity, their physical activity is influenced by their perception of obstacles, specifically the amount of time required for exercise and the time they have available. They overestimate the amount of time needed to achieve fitness and respond by not exercising at all. Sharpe and Connell (1992) found that the level of confidence in one's ability to exercise three times per week was a significant predictor of intention to exercise over the course of the subsequent year. Maintaining health in older adults becomes more difficult as their assessed and perceived abilities for physical activity deteriorates with age.

3.2.5 From Nursing Homes to "Smart Houses"?

The growing population of elderly in the United States and Japan, coupled with increasing life expectancies, means there will likely be increased future demand for products and assistive devices to alleviate mobility problems commonly faced by elders. A recent study by Manton, Corder, and Stallard (1993) showed that use of equipment to assist with physical impairment has increased since 1982. Many seniors develop mobility difficulties that restrict their ability to perform everyday tasks, such as climbing stairs or getting in and out of a bath. Technological products, such as assisting devices, hold the potential for maintaining or increasing quality of life. It is possible that future products for seniors who face mobility restrictions, can help close the gap between life expectancy and quality of life.

Recent technological advancements promise sophisticated solutions to the problems associated with aging.[42] Several authors have noted the potential that "smart house design"[43] and computer technology[44] have in increasing the independence of seniors. The majority of community-living elderly are self-sufficient, with spouses as the main source of support.[45] A lack of family living nearby necessitates help from non-family individuals. Having others close by to assist may subdue or delay the need for a device. However, the demands of living alone may increase the need for a device to help with mobility restriction.

Use of a device is likely to be dependent on need factors. Age, income, and education are characteristics that predispose elders toward device use. Age, through a cohort effect, may influence acceptance of devices. Those in higher income brackets may be better able to afford devices, and those who are better educated may be better able to locate and receive information about devices and how they could be of assistance.

Many seniors have trouble only walking a city block and/or climbing a flight of stairs. Fewer have difficulties getting in and out of the bath and/or getting in and out of a car. However, the majority have difficulty with all 4 tasks. Those with 3 or more of these difficulties are most likely to use a device for assistance. It is usually when the sheer number of problems mount, and not necessarily the severity of those problems, that individuals turn to the use of a device.

3.3 Predisposing Factors in Services Utilization

3.3.1 Widowhood and Social Embeddedness

Recent research suggests that widowhood among elderly hastens death or impairs physical health and leads to hospitalization.[46] Although not all widowed elders experience health declines, many do suffer adverse outcomes. Widowed elders who have deficits in social resources are at greater risk for hospitalizations than widowed persons with adequate social "embeddedness" or perceived social resources.[47] Social embeddedness refers to "the connections that individuals have to significant others in their environment".[48] Perceived social support is the subjective evaluation of the supportive quality of those ties.

Several studies of personal bereavement have shown reductions in the body's immune defenses.[49] Such effects could contribute to an increased risk for hospitalizations among widowed elders. Bereavement may also affect health behaviors. Grief and depression tends to discourage people from maintaining good nutrition[50] and may result in efforts to deny the loss of a spouse through increased consumption of alcohol. Motivation for maintaining good health may suffer if the loss of one's spousal role reduces the purpose and meaning in life.[51] This is often accompanied by a lack of compliance with medical regimes, or restrains on risky health practices.[52] Such changes in health-promoting or health-threatening behaviors exacerbate chronic health problems of the elderly, bringing on an increased likelihood of hospitalizations.

Lack of perceived support has been proposed to be a major contributor to the bereaved's poor health.[53] Resources are most likely to buffer stress when the support available matches the need created by the stressor. The death of the spouse may create a shortage of supportive interchanges that help prevent and deal with health problems. Believing one has a supportive close friend or relative may buffer some of the health consequences of bereavement because the survivor expects such persons to help compensate for the loss of support from the spouse.

Support from friends may be especially important in two ways. First, unlike close relatives, a friend's own distress over the death may not interfere with their helping the widowed elders cope with their loss.[54] Additionally, elders who lack a close friend may be left with no close intragenerational tie after the death of the spouse, and intragenerational ties serve distinctive functions for the well-being of the elderly.[55] Finally, the possible impact of perceived support from children is also relevant, given evidence that solid parent-child relationships after widowhood has been shown to improve the expected length of life among widowed elders.[56]

3.3.2 Health Locus of Control Among Elderly and their Utilization of Health Care Services

The concept of health locus of control refers to the extent to which a person believes his or her health is determined by chance, fate, luck, "powerful" others, or by his or her own efforts. Health locus of control is usually viewed as one of the factors that predisposes individuals to use medical services. Elderly who hold external health locus of control beliefs think that their health is beyond their personal control, and in the control of "powerful" others, especially physicians.[57] Rodin (1986) suggests that this is probably due to some experiences associated with aging which reduces the elderly individual's sense of control. These experiences include loss of friends and family members, and assistance prompted by stereotypes of the elderly as incompetent.

Health locus of control is frequently influenced by health care utilization among the elderly. Hospitalization and nonpreventive physician visits displaces health locus of control from the patient to the physician. Serious medical care use elevates belief in the authority and control of physicians. An increase in physician visits is associated with a displacement of the health locus of control among the elderly, towards doctors and frequently encourages outpatient physician utilization. Thus, utilization of medical services by the elderly increases to some degree because of their increasing faith in doctors as they become older.

3.4 Income of the Elderly as Enabling Factor in Health Care Services Utilization

Enabling factors in health care utilization are described as family or community resources. The essential variable that captures "enablement" is income. Kosloski and Montgomery (1994) have found that elder's income had a statistically significant effect only on the use of home health services.

Bio-medical conditions are the primary factors that affect the length of hospital stay for older patients. However, social factors, such as the availability of informal caregivers, also influences how long an elder remains hospitalized. Informal caregivers can be considered enabling factors because they might either facilitate service use or discourage use of services by meeting the elder's needs directly. The age of the primary caregivers should also be considered. An elder may be hospitalized for a condition that could be treated on an outpatient basis if the age or health of the caregiver allowed for it. On the other hand, a caregiver might request a longer hospitalization if they do not perceive themselves as able to provide the necessary care to the elder upon discharge.

Notes

[8] For detailed reviews see Krause, 1990; Wan, 1989; Wolinsky and Arnold, 1988. For the Manitoba Longitudinal Study on Aging see, Mossey and Shapiro, 1985; Roos, Shapiro, and Tate, 1989. For the Colorado Medicare Study see, McCall and Wai, 1983. For the Health Insurance Plan see, Densen, Shapiro, and Einhorn, 1959. For the Kaiser Permanent System see, McFarland, et al., 1985

[9] There is a great deal of literature on this subject. See, for example, Mossey, Jana and Evelyn Shapiro, "Physician Use by the Elderly Over an Eight year Period", American Journal of Public Health 75, 1985, pp. 133-34; Mutran, Elizabeth and Kenneth F. Ferraro, "Medical Needs and Use of Services Among Older Men and Women", Journal of Gerontology: Social Sciences 43, 1988, pp. s167-71; Ross, Noralou P., Evelyn Shapiro and Leslie L. Ross, Jr., "Aging and the Demand for Health Services: Which Aged and Whose Demand?" The Gerontologist 24, 1984, pp. 31-36; U.S. Senate Committee on Aging, Developments in Aging, 1987: Volume III, The Long Term Care Challenge, February 29, 1988; Waldo, Daniel R., et al., Health Care Financing Review 10:4, Summer 1989, pp. 111-120. Wolinsky Fredric, Ray Mosely and Rodney Coe, "A Cohort Analysis of the Use of Health Services."

[10] See Kenneth F. Ferraro and Thoma T.H. Wan, "Health Needs and Services for Older Adults: Evaluating Policies for the Aging Society", p. 239, in Sidney M. Stahl, editor, The Legacy of Longevity: Health Care in Later Life, Sage Publications, Newbury Park, 1990, pp. 235-254.

[11] Suzanne R. Kunkel and Robert A. Applebaum, Estimating the prevalence of Long-Term Disability for an Aging Society", Journal of Gerontology: Social Sciences 47, 1992, pp. S253-S260. See Table 4 p. S258

[12] Kovar, 1986

[13] Often referred to as the "geriatric imperative"; see Cape, Coe, and Rossman, 1984

[14] Often referred to as the "small group, high use" phenomenon; see Roos, Shapiro, and Tate, 1989

[15] Andersen, 1968; Andersen and Newman, 1973

[16] Bass and Noelker, 1987

[17] Wolinsky, et al., 1990

[18] Wolinsky, et al., 1990

[19] Okun, Stock, Haring, and Witter, 1984

[20] Fozard, Metter, and Brant, 1990

[21] Emery, 1994

[22] Mahler, Rosiello, and Loke, 1986

[23] McSweeny, Grant, Heaten, Adams, and Timms, 1982

[24] Prigatano, Parsons, Wright, Levin, and Hawryluk 1983
[25] Blazer and Williams, 1980
[26] Blazer, Hughes, and George, 1987
[27] Baker and Harvey, 1985
[28] Rice, MacKenzie, and Associates, 1989
[29] Owsley and Sloane, 1990
[30] Lord, Clark, and Webster, 1991
[31] Grisso, et al., 1991
[32] Felson, et al., 1989
[33] Nevitt, Cummings, and Hudes, 1991
[34] Trick and Silverman, 1991
[35] Levit, Lazenby, Cowan, and Letsch, 1991
[36] Bloom, 1982; Bloom, Gift, and Jack, 1992; National Center for Health Statistics, 1960, 1977
[37] Exton-Smith and Overstall, 1979
[38] Badenhop, Cleary, Schaal, Fox, and Bartell, 1983; Bortz, 1980; Harris, Caspersen, De-Firese, and Estes, 1989
[39] deVries, 1970; Tzankoff, Robinson, Pyke, and Brown, 1972
[40] Center for Disease Control, 1989; Fiatarone, et al., 1990; Reavon, Barrett-Conner, and Edelstein, 1991
[41] Caspersen, Cristenson, and Pollard, 1986; Schoenburn, 1986
[42] Bagley and Williams, 1988
[43] Czaja, 1988; La Buda, 1988
[44] Eilers, 1989; Hahm and Bikson, 1989
[45] Stoller and Earl, 1983
[46] Stroebe, Hannson, and Stroebe, 1993
[47] Osterweis, Solomon, and Green 1984
[48] Barrera, 1986, p.415
[49] Irwin and Pike, 1993; Laudenslage and Reite, 1984; Schleifer, Keller, Camerino, Thornton, and Stein, 1983
[50] Perkins and Harris, 1990
[51] Umberson, 1987
[52] Umberson, 1987
[53] Sanders, 1993
[54] Gottlieb and Wagner, 1991
[55] Hochschile, 1978
[56] Silverstein and Bengtson, 1991
[57] Wallston, et. al., 1976

CHAPTER 4

PATERNALISM IN HEALTH CARE FOR THE ELDERLY

4.1 Case of the U.S. Government

The changing demographics of our societies have increasingly focus public and government attention on the problems of the elderly.[58] Spurred by interest group activity, third-party advocacy for the elderly, and the professional concerns of academic gerontologists, the national governments have developed an extensive array of programs designed to ameliorate the biological and psychological changes associated with normal aging.[59] The goals and objectives of the Older Americans Act state that these programs are designed to provide an adequate income in retirement; the best possible physical and mental Health; suitable housing; restorative and community-based, long-term care services; employment opportunities and non-discrimination; retirement in health, honor, and dignity; meaningful participation; efficient community services; immediate benefit from research; and self-determination.[60]

A significant component of the strategy developed to achieve these objectives has been the delivery of social services.[61] Under the Older Americans Act and under Title XX of the Social Security Act, the elderly population in the United States may be eligible for various kinds of supportive services either at home or in the community. The delivery of social services has been increasingly dominated by the medical model; that is, by the redefinition of the problems of aging as primarily medical problems.[62] The primary burden for the provision of support has traditionally rested with the family.[63] When family support is not enough, the elderly population appears to rely on other, informal sources of support.[64] Formal support agencies attempting to provide for any unmet needs have grown over the last few years. The primary authorization and funding for such support comes from the Older Americans Act and from Medicare, Medicaid, and Title XX of the Social Security Act.

For the most part, these services are designed as counterparts to the provision of basic needs such as income, shelter, and food.[65] They cover ancillary needs such as education, recreation, and leisure and also attempt to moderate the normal physical and psychological changes associated with the aging process. Thus recipients may have available to them access-enhancing services, in-home services, legal assistance, congregate meals, and multipurpose senior centers. Moreover, these services tend to emphasize a community-based, continuum of care.

4.2 Case of the Japanese Government

The term 'medical care security' *Iryo Hosho* is used in Japan to refer to one of three functional categories of the contemporary social security system. The other two categories are income security and public welfare services. The Japanese state remains deeply involved in the medical care security system. Provision of medical services has been restricted and regulated according to the Medical Practitioner's law of July 1948. The organization of medical facilities is governed by the Medical Service Law of July 1948, and Japanese citizens not covered by employment based insurance policies are entitled to coverage under the National Health Insurance law of 1958 as amended. In 1957 Prime Minister Tanzan Ishibashi called for the construction of a Japanese welfare-state (*fukushi-kokka*) and the immediate extension of health insurance coverage to the whole population. His successor, Nobusuke Kishi, assumed responsibility for the implementation of the program of `Health Insurance for the Whole Nation' (*Kokumin kai-hoken*) as well as the enactment of other welfare-state measures. Prime Minister Hayato Ikeda in 1960 declared:

> The expansion of social security is an important pillar of the new policy. With the aim of building a welfare state (*fukushi-kokka*), our party has provided health insurance for the whole nation as well as national pensions, but as part of the new policy, an epoch-making expansion of social security will be carried out so as to guarantee that there will not be a single hungry or poverty-stricken person in the nation.[66]

In the early 1960's, Japan constructed a comprehensive network of public annuity and health insurance plans. The benefits of these plans were fairly modest. Toward the end of the high economic growth era around 1970, the Japanese authorities found the annuities and insurance plans attractive political instruments. They wanted to redistribute more income to the elderly, who had not received the full benefits of economic growth, by transforming the plans into inter-generational income-transfer mechanisms. Under intense political pressure, in 1973 the Japanese government made these plans pay very generous benefits to the retired without demanding commitment for the increased burden from the working generation. By the early 1980's, in the midst of an unprecedented fiscal crisis, the Japanese government was forced to announce a state of fiscal emergency and to begin to curtail its expenditures including the programs mentioned above.

The basic concern of the government is not so much the absolute size of the medical cost for the elderly in years to come as it is its size relative to what the working generation will be earning then.[67]

The 'medical care security' system was perceived in Japan as enhancing economic productivity, quality of life for the elderly, political and social stability, and as a way to stimulate domestic demand during a crises in their international balance of payments. This occurred following the 1971 'Nixon shock', when the gold standard was removed. As a result, it elicited great support from Japan's conservative political elite, including both management and labor organizations. In 1973, generally referred to in Japan as 'the first year of welfare' (fukushi gannen), the Japanese government responded to a combination of mass-media and grass roots pressures as well as intra-party rivalry that led to the institution of the truly 'epoch-making' program of virtually free medical care for the elderly.[68]

The institutional paternalism in the provision of social services to the elderly in Japan includes programs based on the law for the Welfare of the Aged of 1963 and the health and Medical Services for the Aged Act of 1982. Through such legislation the government reveals its intentions to take responsibility for the health care needs of its elderly. The growing number of the elderly, though, as a ratio of the whole population, raises serious doubts about the government's ability to meet its paternalistic obligations in the future. In December 1989 the Japanese Ministry of Health and welfare announced its "ten year strategy for the promotion of health and welfare for the elderly." The objective was to enable the elderly to spend the remainder of their lives in good health, free from anxiety and with a sense of purpose. As a result, the Ministry established its "Research Program for Science of Old Age" for the purpose of understanding the aging mechanism and solving such problems as dementia, incontinence and other enfeeblements associated with aging.

4.3   Paternalism in the Medical Community

Along with the State, the health care profession is also taking paternalistic measures in administering health care to the elderly. As a result, recent successful advances in health care have become a double-edged sword. Progress in medical technology can be a resource for extending a healthy and productive life or a means of intervening at the end of life with little regard for the quality of the life that is prolonged. For example, surgical intervention to replace a deteriorated hip joint or to insert a pacemaker may do little to improve the functional health of an 85-year old man who also suffers from advanced cardiopulmonary disease in addition to diabetes, arthritis and dementia. The *technological imperative* of the medical profession, with its emphasis on curing disease, often leads to the use of treatment solely because it is available.[69] Moreover, the use of medicine to prevent death in very ill older patients whose conditions are beyond the hope of cure is an increasingly important variable in health care utilization. As a result, nearly 90 percent of Medicare resources in the U.S. are spent for approximately 5 percent of the older population and most of the costs of health care are devoted to the extended process of dying.[70]

One macro-level model that has been used to explain the provision of services to the elderly is the process of bio-medicalization.[71] The concept of medicalization is used to designate the process by which services for the elderly are increasingly brought under the domain and rationality of medicine; in addition, the elements of the community-sponsored elder services are increasingly drawn toward the provision of medically-related, medically-supportive, and/or medically-oriented services. According to this model, public policy in aging has become dominated by the medical model of analysis and the paternalistic stance of the health care system. The problems associated with aging are diagnosed as medical problems. Under such a system of analysis, the physician becomes the primary gatekeeper to the network of services.[72] These medical gatekeeping functions tends to direct both health and social services toward those recipients with higher levels of medical need.

Notes

[58] Zedlewski, et. al., 1990
[59] Day, 1990
[60] Older American Act, 1965; Estes, 1979; Gelfand, 1988; Olson, 1982
[61] Gelfand, 1988
[62] Binney, Estes, and Ingman, 1990; Estes and Binney, 1989; Robertson, 1990; Smith and Eggelston, 1989
[63] Chapleski, 1989; Coulton and Frost, 1982; Ezell and Gibson 1989; Kaufman, 1990
[64] Ezell and Gibson, 1989
[65] Dobelstein and Johnson, 1985
[66] Jiyu-Minshuto, 1961, p. 657
[67] Ogura, 1994
[68] Steslike, 1991
[69] Weir, 1987
[70] Caplan, 1986
[71] Esten, and Binney, 1989; Robertson, 1990; Binney, et al., 1990:761
[72] Yeo and McGann, 1986

CHAPTER 5

TRENDS IN HEALTH CARE
EXPENDITURES AND FINANCING

5.1 Trends in Health Care Expenditures

On average residents of Japan and the United States have health care expenditures that represent a considerable proportion of their respective GDPs. Table 8 shows a snapshot of the per capita health care expenditure and per capita GDP for the United States and Japan denominated in U.S. dollars for the year 1987.

Table 8

PER CAPITA HEALTH EXPENDITURE AND PER CAPITA GROSS DOMESTIC PRODUCT FOR THE U.S AND JAPAN IN 1987

Country	Per Capita Health Expenditure	Per Capita G.D.P.
U.S.A.	$2,051	$18,338
Japan	$ 915	$13,182

Source: Organization for Economic Cooperation and Development Health Care Systems in Transition, Paris, OECD, 1990.

Health care expenditures in both Japan and the United States have been growing faster than the respective rates of inflation, rates of growth in national income, and rates of population growth. Unusually high growth rates characterize not only the total expenditure on health care, but also the per capita health care expenditures and the health care expenditures as a proportion of GDP. Table 9 indicates that 1960 per capita expenditures on health care were 143 dollars in the United States and 4,400 yen in Japan. By 1990, the respective per capita expenditures were 2,566 dollars and 165,000 yen, an average annual growth rate of 10 percent in the U.S. and 13 percent in Japan.

By comparison, the rate of growth in per capita GDP between 1960 and 1990 was about 2 percent per annum in the United States and 6 percent in Japan.[73] In 1990, the proportion of health care expenditures to GDP was 12.1 percent for the United States and 6.4 percent for Japan, or approximately $1 of health care expenditure for every $8 of GDP in the U.S. and 1 yen of health care expenditure for every 15 yen of GDP in Japan. Since the rate of increase in health care expenditures continues to expand more rapidly than GDP in both countries, health care will continue to represent an increasing share of all final goods and services produced in Japan and the United States.

5.2 Financing Health Care Expenditures

TABLE 9

THE U.S. AND JAPAN TIME TREND
OF HEALTH CARE EXPENDITURES

Year	Total U.S. (millions $)	Total Japan (millions ¥)	Per Capita U.S.	Per Capita Japan	Proportional to GDP U.S. (%)	Proportional to GDP Japan (%)
1960	26,895	480,000	143	4,400	5.23	2.88
1965	41,929	1,465,000	204	11,400	5.98	4.34
1970	74,995	3,339,000	346	24,100	7.43	4.43
1975	132,680	8,378,000	592	57,900	8.38	5.50
1980	248,109	15,749,501	1,063	102,300	9.23	6.42
1985	419,000	21,146,400	1,710	132,300	10.58	6.61
1990	666,187	28,000,000	2,566	165,000	12.08	6.44

Sources: Organization of Economic Cooperation and Development: Health Data File 1992. U.S. Health Care Financing Administration, Health Care Financing Review, Fall 1991.
"National Medical Care Expenditures Estimates," Statistics and Information Department, Ministry of Health and Welfare, Japan.

Financing health care expenditures has become an important issue in the United States and Japan. In 1990, 35 percent of total health care expenditures in the U.S.

was paid for by households, 33 percent by government and 29 percent by business firms. In Japan, health insurance systems cover virtually every person in the country, whether through one of five major schemes for employees and their dependents or through the government livelihood protection system. During the last decade, health care costs continued to grow at an annual rate of 5.9 percent for Japan and 10.4 percent for the U.S. Table 10 shows that rapidly rising costs faced by corporations, households and government agencies are exceeding increases in their ability to fund them.[74]

Especially for businesses and governments in the U.S., the rising health care costs imposes an ever-increasing burden as growth in their ability to finance these costs has failed to keep pace. Japanese health insurance plans have also been faced with similar problems.

While businesses, in the U.S., provide health care coverage for workers and their dependents, governments have emerged as the primary source of health care coverage for the elderly, poor, disabled, and other special disadvantaged groups. In 1990, almost 33 percent of all personal health care expenditures in the U.S. and 39 percent in Japan were consumed by the aged individuals (65 years old and older). These people count for only 12 percent of the population for both countries.

TABLE 10

U.S. HEALTH CARE EXPENDITURES AS A PERCENT OF BUSINESS PROFITS, HOUSEHOLD INCOME, GOVERNMENT REVENUE

Year	Corporate Profits After Tax	Personal Income		Federal Government Revenues	State and Local Government Revenues
		All Ages	65+ years		
	(%)	(%)	(%)	(%)	(%)
1965	14.0	- -	- -	3.5	7.5
1970	36.1	- -	- -	7.3	8.3
1975	34.3	5.1	8.9	11.0	10.2
1980	42.6	- -		11.6	12.6
1985	89.9	- -	- -	14.4	13.5
1990	107.9	5.0	11.5	17.2	6.3

Source: U.S. Health Care Financing Administration, Office of the Actuary: Data from the Office of National Health Statistics, 1991.

5.3 Financing Health Care for Elderly Japan

In Japan the elderly represented 12 percent of the total population in 1987 and consumed 27 percent of the total health care services (Table 11) which represented 7 percent of the GDP. It is expected, though, that by the year 2025 the elderly will represent 23.4 percent of the population in Japan and they will be absorbing 56 percent of all health care services which could represent 13 percent of the GDP.

TABLE 11

TRENDS IN NATIONAL MEDICAL CARE EXPENDITURE FOR THE ELDERLY IN JAPAN

Year	National Expenditures Billion yen	Elderly Expenditures Billion yen	Elderly As A Percentage of National
1975	6,477.9	866.6	13.4%
1980	11,980.5	2,126.9	17.8%
1985	16,015.9	4,067.3	25.4%
1987	18,075.9	4,830.9	26.7%

Source: Japan, Ministry of Health and Welfare, Annual Report, 1990, Table II-1-1.

The free medical care for the elderly policy (introduced in Japan on January 1973) proved to be especially troublesome, as both national and local government finances were strained by the rapid growth in population of those aged 65 and over between 1960 and 1980 (nearly doubling).

During the same period, medical care costs increased by 29 times and the ratio of medical care costs to national income rose from 3.1 percent to 6.0 per cent. In particular, the increased medical care costs of the elderly were striking; a six-fold increase between 1973 and 1981.[75]

By 1982, when the Health Care for the Age Law was enacted, Japan's free medical care for the elderly came to an end. In addition to instituting a small co-payment for those 70 years and older for medical care services, the law provided for the institution of various health promotion and health education programs for the elderly, as well as a plan to integrate medical and social welfare services. More significantly, it instituted a cost-sharing mechanism requiring contributions to the new scheme from existing employment-based insurance schemes[76]. In December 1985 the Ministry of

Health and Welfare enacted an amendment to the Health Services Law mandating formulation of regional medical care plans by prefecture governments. The government urged health policy-makers to adjust the medical care security system to meet the needs and priorities of the 1990's or *minkan katsuryoku or minkatsu for short*. What this amendment prompted was the introduction of the private sector to health care finance. One response to *minkatsu* has been the opening of the health insurance market to both domestic and foreign private insurance products. However, this has neither led to 'dismantling' of the public components of the medical care security structure, nor to wholesale or indiscriminate 'privatization' of the overall system. The privatization that has taken place thus far has been marginal and has not fundamentally altered the public-private balance. The only new changes have been some cost-shifting within the medical security system.[77]

5.4 Financing Health Care for Elderly U.S.A.

In the United States nearly all those aged 65 and older are eligible for Medicare under the Medicare Act of 1965. Although the program provides numerous benefits for the elderly, it leaves many health care needs uncovered. Medicare reimburses the elderly for less than half of all their medical expenses.[78] As a result, in 1990, the elderly in the United States spent, on the average 19 percent of their annual income on health care expenditures and this rate has been on a rising trend.

TABLE 12

HEALTH CARE EXPENDITURES BY THE ELDERLY IN THE UNITED STATES AS A PERCENTAGE OF THEIR ANNUAL INCOME

Year	Percentage
1977	12.3%
1980	12.7%
1984	4.6%
1986	16.0%

Source: House Selected Committee on Aging, "Twentieth Anniversary of Medicare and Medicaid: Americans Still At Risk", Comm. Pub. No. 99-538, Washington, D.C., 1985, Government Printing Office, pp. 4 and 42.

Medicare provides only short-term coverage for acute illnesses. Elderly in need of long-term care for chronic illnesses must become impoverished and then turn to the state for poverty-based assistance. A Senate Committee on Aging reported in

1988 that 90 percent of elderly living along and 66 percent of elderly couples would become impoverished within one year of intensive home care while 70 percent of single elderly persons would become impoverished within 13 weeks of being institutionalized and 50 percent of married couples would become impoverished within six months of one spouse being institutionalized.[79]

In 1988, 5.7 million elderly in the United States needed long-term health care services. In one national sample of nursing home admissions, 35 percent of the elderly who applied for admission were earning less than $1,104 a month and as a result were eligible for Medicaid upon admission to the nursing home.[80] The remaining nursing home patients who enter as private-paying, subsequently spend down all of their savings, become impoverished and therefore become eligible for Medicaid.[81]

In 1988, Medicaid expenditures consumed between 10 percent to 15 percent of state budgets,[82] and the spousal impoverishment provisions from the federal government were estimated at $651 million for 1990 and $1.6 billion for 1992.[83]

This situation is critical for many elderly persons and their families and for both state and federal budgets. The number of elderly as a percent of the total population, in both the United States and Japan is expected to double in the next three decades. This increase will deteriorate the current problem of health care financing. An equally important problem to the problem of financing will be the problem of resource allocation for both national economies. When a society has a given income and more of this income is absorbed year after year to finance the production of health care as a consumer's good, then less income becomes available to finance the production of other goods, especially investment goods which are needed for economic growth.

5.5 Health Care Price Inflation

A contentious issue is the inflation component of medical expenditures that reveals that people pay more for health care services over time not because they are using more services but because they are charged more for the same services.

The annual compound increase in health care prices between 1975 and 1987 was 4.1 percent for Japan and 8.1 percent for the U.S. During the same time period the compound increase in the prices of everything else produced in the country was 2.9 percent for Japan and 5.8 percent for the U.S. Table 13 indicates that during the 1975-1987 period, the increase in the annual compound rate of health care prices has been 41.4 percent higher than the increase in the annual compound rate in the prices of all final goods and services produced in Japan and 37.9 percent higher than the increase in the annual compound rate in the prices of all final goods and services produced in the U.S.

TABLE 13

INFLATION MEASURES (1975-1987)

Country	Health Care Price Deflator	GDP Deflator	Excess Health Care Inflation
Canada	8.6	6.5	2.0
France	7.6	8.8	-1.1
Germany	3.9	3.4	0.4
Italy	14.9	14.1	0.7
Japan	4.1	2.9	1.2
United Kingdom	10.8	9.7	1.0
United States	8.1	5.8	2.2
Mean	8.3	7.3	0.9

Source: Organization for Economic Cooperation and Development: Health Data File, 1989.

5.6 Financing of Rising Health Care Prices

How problematic is it for a society to be charged more for the same health care services year after year and how long can that society afford to pay the rising bill? When we apply this question to the case of the unproductive aged, then the real problem becomes an issue of higher budgets. This concern is exacerbated by the aging of the population and its implications for more intensive and extensive use of health care resources in the future. Concern about higher budget persists in Japan and the U.S. because of continuing economic constraints coupled with competing pressures in the use of resources.

Financing of health care services for the aged is not always automatic, as it would be under a full market system in which price both brought supply and demand into equilibrium and provided the funding via the care supplied. When the public share in health care financing for the aged is significant, then decisions about spending on health care become political. In such cases, the main concern is the Leu effect;[84] not only an oversupply in health care services for the aged but an oversupply at inflated cost. The possibility of a Leu effect dramatizes the issue of financing. The retired aged earn no current income from present activities. Therefore, only their life savings and those who consider caring for them will pay the price. If the elderly use more health care services at inflated prices than what they actually can finance themselves, then, our societies will have to keep transferring more and more resources from the productive sectors to pay the bill.

Both, in the U.S. and Japan there is an element, often a large element of tax financing. Tax financing of medical expenditures comes, though, with well-known inefficiencies and expansion of the medical sector will expand such inefficiencies.[85] Medicaid in the U.S. is tax financed and that is true for part of Medicare. In Japan a law of health and Medical Services for the Elderly was enforced as of February 1st, 1983. With a view to having the burden of costs shared equitably by the whole population, the amount excluding cost-sharing by the elderly is borne 20 percent by the state and 5 percent each by the prefectures and municipalities, while the remaining 70 percent is contributed by the insured of the various medical care insurance schemes.

Rising prices for health care services will unavoidably result into higher budgets for health insurance companies and for both the federal government and municipalities. Forcing an increasing share of GDP to flow through government channels rather than the private sector of the economy will be a seriously unattractive project. If tax financing of health care services for the aged proves unacceptable in the future then real outlays on health care services for the elderly could fall with a devastating impact on the aging society.

Notes

[73] A detailed accounting of national health care expenditures for the U.S. appears in Health Care Financing Review, 11:4, 1990. For a comparison with Japan see George   J. Scheiber and Jean-Pierre Poullier, "International Health Care Expenditure Trends", Health Affairs, 8:3, Fall 1989, pp. 169-177; and "Overview of International Comparisons of Health Care Expenditures," Health Care Financing Review, Annual Supplement 1989, pp 1-7.

[74] See Katherine R. Levit, and Cathy A. Cowan, "Business, Households, and Government: Health Care Costs, 1990", Health Care Financing, Vol. 13, No. 2, 1991, pp. 83-93

[75] Ishimoto, 1989

[76] Steslicke and Kimura, 1985

[77] Steslicke, 1991

[78] Brown, 1984

[79] Senate Committee on Aging, 1988, p. 30

[80] Leu, Doty and Manton, 1990

[81] Senate Committee on Aging, 1988, p. 37

[82] Senate Committee on Aging, 1988, p. 36

[83] Harrington and Quadagno, 1990, p. 266

[84] Leu, R.R., "The Public-Priate Mix and International Health Care Costs", in Cylyer, A.J. and Jonsson, B. eds., Public and Private Health Services: Complementarities and Conflicts, Basil Blackwell, Oxford, England 1986.

[85] See Browning Edgar, "On the Marginal Welfare Cost of Taxation", American Economic Review 77, 1987, pp. 11-23; Ballard, Charles John Shoven and John Whalley, "General Equilibrium Computations of the Marginal Welfare Costs of Taxes in the United States", American Economic Review 75, 1985, pp. 128-138; Stuart, Charles, "Welfare Costs per Dollar of Additional Tax Revenue in the United States", American Economic Review 74, 1984, pp. 352-362

CHAPTER 6

OUR APPROACH TO THE PROBLEM

In the U.S., 83 percent of the annual rate of growth of health care expenditures is a result of higher prices for the purchase of the same level of health care services. For Japan, the rate is 45 percent. Health care providers in both countries consistently keep charging higher prices for the same services year after year. This price instability is a result of the way costs and prices relate to labor productivity in the health care services sector, and is the main focus of our model.

6.1 Productivity and Wages

TABLE 14
LABOR PRODUCTIVITY IN HEALTH CARE SERVICES

Year	Patient Consultations & Visits to Health Care Providers in Thousands (a)		Total Health Care Employment: Number of Persons or Man Years in Thousands (b)		Labor Productivity in Health Care Sector (a/b)	
	U.S.	Japan	U.S.	Japan	U.S.	Japan
1970	1,004,754	1,410,592	2,878	1,032	349	1,366
1975	1,101,462	1,661,648	4,046	1,335	272	1,244
1980	1,093,233	1,681,920	5,119	1,724	213	975
1985	1,244,250	1,533,250	6,142	1,824	202	840

Source: Organization for Economic cooperation and Development: Health Data File, 1989, Paris 1990.

Labor productivity is a measure of real output per unit of labor input. Table 14 calculates labor productivity in the health care sector by dividing patient consultations and visits to health care providers by total employment in the health sector in man-years using OECD data. The calculation indicates that labor productivity, as defined here, has been declining in both, the U.S. and Japan, during the 1970-1985 period. More labor hours have been used by health care providers to produce the same level of health care services. For consumers this implies a quality improvement of health care services over time since more attention (more labor hours) are devoted to each patient consultation. For health care providers, though, this implies an increase in unit production costs. An increase in unit labor costs (that is, labor cost per unit of output) approximates the difference between the increase in nominal-wage rates and the increase in labor productivity. More precisely:

Percentage Change in Labor Cost	=	Percent Change in Nominal Wage Rate	-	Percent Change in Productivity

6.1.1 Compensating Health Care Providers

Even if nominal wages by health care providers are kept unchanged, when labor productivity of health care providers declines, then labor cost per unit of output will increase. The labor cost per unit of output in the health sector will also increase if the income of health care providers grows faster than their labor productivity. This is the focus of our model. When the labor cost per unit of output for the health care providers grows positively over time then prices for health care services will grow by the same rate. That is, health care providers pass on the higher unit labor costs in the form of higher prices for services. Otherwise, the per unit of output cost increase in health care services can be eliminated by either increasing the labor productivity in health care services or by eliminating the wage increase of health care providers. The first option is unfeasible given the nature of health care service, and the second is undesirable for reasons described below.

6.1.2 Labor Productivity Growth in the Health Services Industry

Labor productivity growth in health care services is inherently slow for two reasons. As William Baumol[86] puts it, health services are resistant to standardiza-tion. Before a patient is cured it is necessary for the health care provider to deter-mine, case by case, what is the health problem of the patient and the treatment must then be tailored to the individual case. A second reason why it has been difficult to reduce the labor content of health care services is the fact that quality is believed to be inescapably correlated with the amount of labor expended on their production. The health industry has taken large steps in improving the quality of services over time, but while the amount of physician time spend per patient-visit or per illness has declined somewhat, it has done so only marginally. Productivity improvement in the provision of health care services has been small and insignificant. When taking into consideration the fact that over time each patient-visit requires more and more labor input by adding to the physician the labor services of secretaries who make appointments, nurses who prepare patients for the physician's interview, bookkeepers who maintain accounts receivable and bill insurance companies, etc., then the overall labor productivity will be declining in the health care sector over time. Competition among health care providers makes sufficient labor productivity improvement unattainable for the health care sector.

An important implication of this reality is the following: When labor productivity is declining over time, then price stability for the output of health care services can be attained only by a declining nominal income for health care providers. Reducing, or event keeping the nominal income of health care providers unchanged over time is practically impossible because of the rising real income in productivity progressive industries. Labor productivity in many industries has been increasing steadily as a result of automation, standardization and wage incentives. If output per man-hour in manufacturing industries increases by, say, 3 percent per year and management in these industries agrees to a matching rise in labor wages and bonuses (wages and bonuses go up by 3 percent) then the labor cost per unit of output (the ratio between total labor cost and total output) remains absolutely unchanged (cost per unit of output remains stationary) and there is no need for output prices of such manufactured products to rise in order to maintain company profits. Management has no reason to refuse matching of wages to productivity increases because such wage increases leave labor cost per unit of output unaffected and have no impact on a firm's competitiveness.

Management matches wages and bonuses to labor productivity increases in an effort to obtain and maintain productivity gains.[87] As Ferber and Loed (1974:69) have argued, "One of the basic tenets of the private enterprise system is that income should be distributed according to contribution." One of the themes that has come to dominate both the more general literature on reward allocation and the literature on pay in organizations is precisely the connection between pay and performance.[88] Several prominent economic theories also emphasize the importance of productivity in determining earnings. In the neoclassical economic tradition, human capital theory emphasizes the connection between productivity and earnings.[89] A productivity leading sector can afford raising wages without suffering a per unit of output cost increase and therefore without being forced to increase the price of its final product to maintain company profits. Such an industry policy, though, can have important

...plications for lagging or stagnant labor productivity sectors such as health care services.

Increasing wages in the productivity leading sectors change the relative purchasing power of the wages in the productivity lagging or stagnant sectors. For health care providers to maintain the relative purchasing power of their income over time, their wages should keep increasing by the same rate as the wages of the productivity leading sectors. Since such an increase is not matched by an increase in labor productivity, the per unit of output cost of health care services will increase and the prices of these services will have to keep increasing.

6.1.3 Health Care Cost-Containment Through Price Ceilings

The only way to prevent price inflation in this sector would be by imposing a price ceiling on the output of health care providers.[90] Such an option, though, is undesirable. Stabilizing the prices of health care providers through a price ceiling on health care services could bring about exactly the opposite result from the one originally intended.[91] If rising prices merely reflect real and unavoidable cost increases, a ceiling in the prices of health care services will inevitably serve, in the long run, to curtail the supply of medical services in general; and a ceiling on fees for the treatment of the elderly is sure to reduce the quality and quantity of services supplied to this population group. In the long run, it may even increase the prices the elderly will be required to pay because of their increased demand for health care services and the reduced supply. Price control on health care services would constitute no benefit to the group of persons they are intended to protect in a market economy.

In sum, the price of the output generated by the productivity leading sectors can be stabilized but the price of the output generated by the productivity lagging or stagnant sectors will have to keep rising. A persisting inflationary pressure in the prices of health care services is unavoidable if health providers should be successful in resisting erosion of their real income in the short run and societies should be successful in maintaining a desired quantity and quality of health care services in the long run.

6.2 The Source of Health Care Inflation

Although the controversial discussion on health care occasionally attempt to address the causes of inflation in this industry, we hold that the true cause of the rising health care costs is the increase in wages and incomes of those working in the productivity-*leading* sectors of the economy (those with consistent positive productivity growth). As productivity in these sectors rises, management agrees to a matching rise in the wages and bonuses, since it will not effect the per unit of output labor cost. This leads to a relative erosion of incomes in productivity-*lagging* sectors, and health care is one of them.

For consumers, health care services, as discussed, is an inelastic good: as the price of services rises, the demand for them does not decline, or it does so only marginally. Therefore, health care providers are always successful in resisting erosion of their relative incomes by securing for themselves an increase in nominal incomes of at least the same as the nominal wages of the productivity-*leading* sectors. Higher labor costs in the health care sector, however, are not accompanied by higher productivity. As a result, the per unit labor costs of production rise at the same rate as the rise in nominal wages. Administrators cover this increase in wages by raising the price of their services and thereby pass on the added labor cost per unit of output to the consumers, insurance companies and to a large extent, the government. As the principle of price inelasticity would suggest, these higher prices, unmatched with a decrease in demand, would raise revenue for the health care sector. Thus, passing on the productivity gains in the productivity-leading sectors in the form of higher wages and incomes to those employed by them, eventually inflates the prices of services from productivity lagging sectors such as health care. Historically, this tendency has been systematic[92] as many studies suggest.

In order to address the acceleration of health care costs, it is necessary to simulate how the wage pressure-component of health care inflation and the growing aging population will effect the industry as well as other more productive industries. But doing so requires care attention to wages and prices in both sectors of the economy and labor transformation from one sector to the other. It also calls for detailed assumptions concerning production and consumption. Our model recognizes this scrutiny in detail and shows that under different productivity assumptions for both the U.S. and Japan, our economies are able to support the continually escalating healthcare costs as long as we maintain adequate productivity levels in other sectors of the economy.

The idea of explaining the "cost disease"[93] of health care services in terms of labor productivity, per unit of output labor cost and prices has the important implication of the following: *Health care services in our society can indeed withstand the growing demand of the aging population, even though the price of services doubles, as long as productivity in all other sectors rises at a consistent rate.* The U.S. and Japan will be able to afford the increasing costs of health care brought on by the aging population as long as productivity gains are transferred properly to the health care sector via a freedom of labor mobility and equal wage increases. Personal income in both sectors will increase, and the relative share of the population in the labor force will decrease. Consumers will be able to afford the same as before, including increasingly expensive healthcare, and both economies are able to support their growing health care sector.

6.3 Technological Improvements in the Medical Industry

Besides higher labor costs, another costly component to health care has been the rising growth in capital-related factors, or high-tech medical equipment. Throughout the last 40 years the accumulation of capital in this industry has surpassed that of most other industries in the economy. The standard assumption associated with a higher capital input to production is that the productivity for the labor input will increase, and hence a lower proportion of labor would go into production. This can be best illustrated with the *automation* of such industries as automobiles and semiconductors where the *returns* to capital investment can easily be measured.

The health industry is unique in that while the industry has indeed benefited from the increase in technological equipment, it has not necessarily done so in a quantitative way. The health industry has, however, reaped qualitative benefits from capital investment in that our quality of living has improved dramatically from advances in medical technology and our average life expectancy has increased. This development has been what we call a *health care paradox* in that the more that is invested in capital equipment, the better the treatment we receive; our quality of life improves and we enjoy a longer average life expectancy. The longer our life expectancy, the more health care we consume in our aged years. Diseases that were once considered terminal are now long-term. Thus, we place an ever higher strain on our labor resources in that more labor must be transferred away from more productive sectors and into health care. Moreover, our economy allows for the wages of this labor group to rise in line with those in the more productive sectors. As we have shown above, higher wages unmet with productivity growth, increases the costs in health care far faster than in the productive sectors.

The growing aging population in both the United States and Japan is evidence that this paradox is a reality. The only fields that have seen continuous job growth even over the last few recessionary years are those related to health care. In the United States alone, less than 9.02 million were employed in the aggregate health services industries in 1994. As of May 1995, 9.28 million were employed in these health services.[94] Over this selected 12 month period, employment growth averaged roughly 20,000 new jobs a month or 1 percent.

Although this issue can be discussed at great length, we do not focus our model on it. However, this quality versus quantity component of capital in the health sector will simplify our model. We argue that all capital growth in the medical field has not affected the productivity of the health industry, but has only improved the quality of *output*. In other words, this sector is *capital-neutral*. We use labor as the only input to production. Thus, we can circumvent the controversy of allocating capital in an economy with limited capital resources.

The current system in place suggests that tax financing of health care services for the aged is necessary. If so, the additional tax revenue can be raised from the productivity gains in the productivity-leading sectors. These gains, distributed in the form of higher wages, can be partially transferred to the public sector for the provision of affordable health care services for the growing elderly class. As long as the economy sustains the productivity level in the non-health sector, the transferability of resources is feasible and the economy can support its aging population. However, the ways and means by which resources are transferred to support this segment of the population (the form or incidence of tax) is subject to much controversy, and is not modeled here. We recognized that this issue is no less important than many that we do discuss, but we leave the discussion of this issue to the policy makers.

6.4 Empirical Estimates of Productivity Growth Rates in the United States and Japan

A number of empirical estimates of productivity growth rates in the United States and Japan are byproducts of estimates of economic growth models by various researchers.[95] Another set of estimates is a result of total factor productivity estimates by a number of researchers.[96] Table 15 below lists one set of productivity estimates from OECD data.

Table 15 indicates that the Japanese economy outperformed the United States in terms of business output growth up to the middle 1980s. For the period before 1973, a rough estimate would assign somewhat more than one-half of Japan's economic growth to Total Factor Productivity (TFP) and most of the balance to capital input, with only a small fraction attributed to labor input. After 1973, growth slowed dramatically, and the importance of TFP growth declined while that of capital increased, a phenomenon that also occurred in the United States.Japan experienced a rapid rate of growth of output and capital input, while the United States experienced a strong growth in labor input.

TABLE 15

REAL GROSS PRODUCT, FACTOR INPUTS AND PRODUCTIVITIES IN THE BUSINESS ECONOMIES OF THE U.S. AND JAPAN 1960-1973, 1973-1979 AND 1979-1986
(Percentage Rates of Change)

Country	Real Gross Business Product (a) + (b)	Factor Inputs			Factor Productivity		
		Total	Labor (a)	Capital	Total	Labor (b)	Capital
United States:							
1960-73	3.8%	2.3%	1.7%	3.5%	1.5%	2.2%	0.3%
1973-79	2.8%	2.9%	2.5%	3.7%	-0.1%	0.3%	-0.9%
1979-86	2.2%	2.2%	1.6%	3.3%	0.0%	0.6%	-1.0%
Japan:							
1960-73	9.7%	3.5%	1.0%	12.1%	6.1%	8.6%	-2.4%
1973-79	3.8%	2.0%	0.6%	6.8%	1.8%	3.2%	-3.0%
1979-86	3.8%	2.1%	1.0%	5.8%	1.7%	2.8%	-2.0%

Source: Englander and Mittelstadt (1988), based on the national source data and Organization for Economic Cooperation and Development estimates.

Table 16 indicates that during the 1985-90 period, the U.S. productivity growth was up from 2 percent to 2.7 percent, compared with the previous period. In Japan, productivity growth increased from 4.5 to 5.5 percent. In the 1990-93 period, U.S. productivity rose 2.5 percent per year while Japan suffered the most severe decline in its growth rate compared with the previous period - from 5.5 percent to less than 2 percent annually.

TABLE 16

ANNUAL PERCENTAGE CHANGE IN MANUFACTURING
PRODUCTIVITY UNIT LABOR COSTS AND RELATED MEASURES
(Selected periods, 1979-1993)

	Output Per Hour	Unit Labor Costs	Total Output	Employment	Hourly Compensation
United States:					
1979-93	2.4	1.5	-0.8	-1.1	5.3
1979-85	2.0	0.7	-1.2	-1.4	6.9
1985-90	2.7	2.8	0.0	-0.1	3.9
1990-93	2.5	1.2	-1.3	-1.9	4.3
Japan:					
1979-93	4.3	4.5	0.3	0.9	4.6
1979-85	4.5	5.8	1.1	1.2	4.7
1985-90	5.5	5.8	0.4	0.8	4.7
1990-93	1.8	0.0	-1.7	0.8	4.3

Source: M. Greiner, C. Kask, and C. Sparks. "Comparative Manufacturing Productivity and
Unit Labor Costs." Monthly Labor Review, February 1995, p. 30.

In the 1979-93 period, Japan's productivity gains were due entirely to rising output. Productivity growth in the United States was due more to reductions in labor input. Manufacturing output in the United States increased at a rate of 1.5 percent annually between 1979 and 1993. Manufacturing output grew on average 4.5 percent in Japan. Japan's rate of growth was 5.5 percent from 1979 to 1991, but output declined in 1992 and 1993. U.S. manufacturing employment declined at a rate of 1 percent annually between 1979 and 1993. In Japan, it increased at a rate of about 1 percent annually during this period. More specifically, employment in the United States fell 1.5 percent annually during the 1979-85 period, was unchanged between 1985 and 1990, and decreased about 2 percent annually from 1990 to 1993. In Japan, employment increased by about 1 percent per year in each of the three periods. Hourly compensation costs in the U.S. manufacturing rose at an average rate of 5.3 percent per year during the 1979-93 period, while in Japan the hourly compensation growth was 4.5 percent annually. In Japan, strong productivity growth almost completely offset hourly compensation increases, resulting in unit labor costs that were nearly flat over the 1979-93 period. The average unit labor cost growth in the United States was less than 3 percent annually during this period. Between 1979 and 1993, with each country's unit labor costs measured on a national currency basis, U.S. unit labor costs rose by about 2 percent per year relative to Japan. The growth rate of unit labor costs in the United States decelerated from about 5 percent between 1979 and 1985 to about 1 percent between 1985 and 1990. During this period, Japan's unit labor cost growth rates were lower than in the United States.

Productivity growth represents the means by which the effects of input price increases may be mitigated, and the means by which payments to factors of production may rise without increasing prices.

This interesting relationship between the unit labor cost equation and the labor productivity equation indicates that additional information on health care expenditures can be drawn from productivity measures. We are now able to look directly at the movement of health care output prices and then analyze the movement in terms of the prices of labor inputs, as they are directly linked to productivity growth rates in other sectors. Our model draws assumptions of productivity growth from the above tables, and generates simulations for the next few decades of productivity growth, labor costs and prices for health services. Thus, we analyze trends in health care output prices in terms of input prices and productivity.

Notes

[86] Baumol, William J., "Private Affluence, Public Squalor", Economic Research Report no. 92-15, C.V. Starr Center for Applied Economics, New York University, April, 1992.

[87] Yellen, 1984; Katz, 1986

[88] Medoff and Abraham, 1980; Bishop, 1987; Kanter, 1987; Baker, Jensen, and Murphy, 1988, Konrad and Pfeffer, 1990

[89] Becker, 1962, 1964; Mincer, 1970; Frank, 1984

[90] For an interesting discussion on this subject see: Ikegami, Naoki, "Japanese Health Care: Low Cost Through Regulated Fees.", Health Affairs 10:8, 1991, pp. 87-109; Levy, Jesse, et al., "Impact of the Medical Fee Schedule on Payments to Physicians", Journal of the American Medical Association 264, 1990, pp. 717-722; McGuire, Thomas G., and Mark Pauly, "Physician Response to Fee Changes with Multiple Players", Journal of Health Economics 10, 1991; U.S. Select Committee on Aging, H.R., Less Profit, Less Care? Reassessing the Impact of Medicare and Medicaid Cuts on Patients, Vol. 1, 2., Government Printing Office, Washington, D.C., 1988.

[91] See: Baumol, W.J., "Price Controls for Medical Services and the Medical Needs of the Nations Elderly", Paper commissioned by the American Medical Association and presented to the Physician Payment Review Commision, March 18, 1988.

[92] Krugman, Baumol, et al.

[93] Among the first writings to offer such an analysis was Baumol, W.J. and W.G. Bowen, Performing Arts: The Economic Dilemma, Twentieth Century Fund, New York, 1966

[94] Source: the U.S. Department of Labor

[95] This group contains the estimates of Crisensen, Cummings and Jorgenson 1976); Denison and Chnug (1976); and Nishimizu and Hulten (1978).

[96] Estimates are from studies done by Baumol (1986); Baumol, Blackman and Wolff (1989); Cristensen, Cummings and Jorgenson (1981); Dollar and Wolff (1988); Englander and Mittelstadt (1988); Hulten (1990); Jorgenson and Griliches (1967); Jorgenson, Kuroda and Nishimizu (1987); Kendrick (1961 and 1985); Nadiri (1970); Norsworthy and Malmquist (1983); and the U.S. Department of Labor (1983).

CHAPTER 7

THE SIMULATION MODEL

The following mechanism is expected to be at work.

1) Incomes in the health care sector will continue rising but labor resources will be transferred from the productivity-progressive sector to the productivity-stagnant sector at a rate that is consistent with freedom of labor mobility and equality of wages.

2) Output and incomes in the productivity leading sectors will rise at the same rate while inputs, namely labor, will decline in the leading sector.

3) Output of the productivity-stagnant sector will keep growing as the aging population rises, demand for health services rises and more inputs (labor) are added to its production

4) More health care services will be provided at increasing prices but our societies will be able to afford these services as long as productivity in the progressive sectors keeps rising at a consistent rate.

Four separate simulations of our model with different parameters used to represent productivity growth show that the above scenario is feasible. Both the U.S. and Japan can finance the rising costs of health care services in the future.

7.1 Simplified Version of Model

Since, as discussed, the health industry has not seen significant quantitative returns to its capital, we can focus our model purely on the labor input to the economy. We simplify our model by eliminating capital as an input and measuring just the labor input to production.

Appendix I provides a more formal presentation of the interrelationships between the non-health sectors and the health care sector. A two-sector, two-good, single input (labor) production and consumption model is given. Standard maximization techniques of the model generate the interrelationships between inputs and outputs, prices and wages, consumption and prices, productivity and wages, and the transfer of labor and output. We calculate the "market value of" output that refers to the price of the good in question multiplied by that variable. Since this is a two-sector, two-good economy, there are only two prices, but the model holds the price in the non-health sector fixed in order to measure the relative price of health care over time. No currency enters the model, even though prices do. Thus, the "market value" of output is given in units, not dollars or Yen. The model is written at the graduate level but detailed explanation is provided throughout the appendix.

7.2 Some Basic Concepts

Initial conditions are given for all variables, and most of these variables are determined by the set of assumptions. Our first assumption, that labor productivity rates and the aging ratio are all assumed to grow at a constant and pre-determined rate, will establish the *exogenous* variables. These variables are exogenous as they are set independent of the other variables. All the other variables such as wages, prices, output or expenditures, GDP and the labor force allocation between sectors are all computed as a function of one or more variables as the appendix illustrates. This second set of variables are *endogenous* since they are determined within the confines of the model. It is important to keep these two concepts in mind as the simulation results are explained.

The model has been simulated for both the U.S. and Japan to project the future trends of wages, prices and output as well as labor resource allocation between the health sector and the rest of the economy, given the predetermined rate of productivity growth in both sectors. An elaborate set of initial conditions is provided reflecting outstanding values of the indicators in question, indexed in some circumstances for simplification of the model. The goal of these simulations is to project future costs, relative wages and the changing labor resources given the assumptions listed below.At issue is the fact that the size of the aging population has grown dramatically over the past years and this trend is expected to continue. The costs of financing health care for this segment of the population requires considerable planning on the part of the rest of the economy. Allocating resources properly and efficiently will enable our societies to finance this growing sector as the model will demonstrate.

Although separate simulations were run using different initial assumptions for either the U.S. or Japan's productivity rate, no interaction of activity is assumed between the U.S. and Japan. The model is based on many functions or relationships between different variables such as productivity, wages and prices, but no such functional relationships exist between Japan's variables and those of the U.S. or vice versa. A global economy used for macroeconomic model studies would assume a relationship between the two countries' economies. However, this is a micro-economic model. Both sets of simulations are run using a different set of initial conditions as a comparison of the two economies from the current circumstances to the future. As a result, no exchange rate system is included in the model.

7.3 Variables

Only the variables listed below are measured from 1990 to 2025.

Variable	Symbol
Population	N
Output	Q
Market Value of Output	Y
Labor Force	L
Retired	L_r

Variable	None-health Sector	Health Sector
Wage	W	W
Productivity	D_1	D_2
Price	P_1	P_2
Per Capita Labor	l_1	l_2
Per Capita Output	q_1	q_2
Market Value of per capita Output	y_1	y_2

7.4 General Assumptions

The seven assumptions listed below are based on general microeconomics principals and our assumptions concerning the future state of the economy with par-ticular focus on the health care industry.

1) The main structure of the model is built on the premise of a dual sector econ-omy: the non-health sector and the health sector. The health sector, sector B,

provides health care services which will be called health care output. The non-health sector, sector A, provides for all other goods and services needed in our society.

2) Labor productivity in the non-health sector is progressive and in the health sector is stagnant. The productivity growth rate for the non-health sector is higher than the health sector. The wage growth rate for both sectors is constant and predetermined for the time period being considered.

3) The labor force is homogenous in the two sectors allowing for freedom in labor mobility from one sector to the other with no transitional costs. As a result, the wage rate is identical in both sectors. This is a standard assumption in production models similar to this. Homogeneity implies that all employees within one sector have the same productivity. When moving from one sector to another, an employee takes on the productivity of that sector.

    The reader is encouraged to consult a graduate level microeconomics textbook such as Varian, Mansfield, Salvatore, Shotter, or a labor economics textbook such as Enherenberg and Smith, for a better understanding of this material.

4) Total GDP is equal to the sum of the market values of outputs in the two sectors (the output of the non-health sector multiplied by the price of the output, plus the output of the health sector multiplied by its price). Total GDP is equal to the national income (the wage rate in each sector multiplied by the labor force). This follows the basic tenet used to measure GDP and the national income in a single input economy.

5) The total population is equal to the total labor force plus retirees. "Population" is defined as the noninstitutional civilian labor force aged 16 years or over. All retirees are those 65 years or older. The ratio of retirees to the whole population, called the aging population, is assumed to grow at a constant rate. Table 2 shows the actual and expected aging ratio for both the U.S. and Japan from 1950 to 2050, and it is from here that we derive the annual rate of growth of the aging population for both Japan and the U.S.

6) Total production equals total consumption as GNP equals national income. In other words, there is no savings, no investment and no inventories.

7) There is no unemployment. All members of the population who are not retirees
    are in the labor force employed in one of the two sectors. As a result the labor
    force participation rate is very high compared to national statistics.

Note, the simulations are done on a per capita basis. Since many variables are
denominated by N (the total population) many complicated issues are circumvented.
For example, the model does not address population booms or busts or demographic
differences. It merely assumes a rising aging ratio in relation to the labor force; that
is, less of the population is in the labor force over time. Secondly, although the
simulations show a falling labor-input in the non-health sector, it only represents a
falling labor ratio in that sector brought on by productivity gains. It is trivial to
demonstrate that the rising rate of the aging population must equal the growth in the
labor-input to the health sector less the fall in the labor-input of the non-health sector.

7.5 Data-specific Initial Conditions

In keeping the simulations of the model more in line with current conditions in
both the U.S. and Japan's economies, we take some values for our initial conditions
from empirical studies. The variables that can be supported include productivity, the
proportion of the aging population and the ratio of the market value of health output
to total output. However, in order to keep the model consistent throughout, it was
necessary for us to come up with arbitrary assumptions concerning the initial value
of other variables such as prices and wages.

We do not specify the term *output* in either sector. For example, Table 14 reports the number of patient consultants per health care employee. We do not adhere
to this definition but instead derive a quasi-output (q_i or i=1 and 2 in each sector
from labor allocation in that sector and productivity). The production function is
linear according to the following:

$$q_i = D_i l_i \text{ , where i represents the two sectors.}$$

Following this assumption and those for the initial conditions, we can derive
output and total GDP.

The derivation of the variables is described more thoroughly in the appendix.
In this study, we focus more on the *growth* rate of the variables, and less on the levels. Nevertheless, below we provide the data-specific initial conditions starting in
the year 1990.

1) *Aging Ratio:* The average annual growth rate of the elderly from the year 1990 to 2025 is expected to be 1.95 percent for Japan and 1 percent for the U.S. These estimates are based on the data presented in Table 2: The percentages of aged people - those 65 years or older - to the population in 1990 were 11.9 percent for Japan and 12.6 percent for the U.S. A Japanese forecast for this group for the year 2025 is 23.4 percent making the annual growth rate for the elderly in Japan equal to 1.97 percent.

$$\left[\left(\frac{23.4}{11.9} \right)^{(1/35\ years)} - 1 \right] = 1.95 \text{ percent}$$

In the U.S., the aging ratio for the year 2025 is estimated at 17.9 percent   (See Table 2), making the annual growth rate of the elderly for the U.S. equal to 1 percent.

$$\left[\left(\frac{17.9}{12.6} \right)^{(1/35\ years)} - 1 \right] = 1 \text{ percent}$$

The standard error for these projections is small and insignificant. Note, although the growth rate in the U.S. will tend to accelerate when the baby boomers hit 65 which starts in the year 2010, this is reflected in the projected ratio in 2025. The model assumes a constant annual growth rate for simplicity.

2) *Labor Productivity:* In the U.S., Labor productivity has been higher than that in Japan. It is assumed that for 1990, the labor productivity in the non-health sector is 2.06 for the U.S. and 2.00 for Japan, while in the health sector it is 1.29 and 1.25 for the U.S. and Japan respectively. Note, a productivity of 2 represents 2 units of output per worker. These estimates are analogous to those estimated by the empirical literature. Below, we define the term *output* (see item 7). Although these are used as our initial conditions, we focus on the productivity growth rates which are 3 percent per year in Japan and 2 percent per year in the U.S. for non-health and less than this for the health sector in both countries.

3) *Wage Rate:* Wages in the U.S. are slightly higher than those in Japan. For 1990 the average wage rate in Japan is assumed to be $10.00 per hour while that in the U.S. is assumed to be $10.30 per hour. Wage rates grow at the same rate as labor productivity in the non-health sector based on the discussion of the per

unit labor costs of production in section 6.1. The labor force is homogeneous allowing for free mobility of labor between sectors.

4) *Prices:* Since we are interested in the relative price of health care, we can assume that the price in the non-health sector remains constant, while the price of the health sector is higher initially (in 1990), and keeps rising over time. This is also consistent with the difference in productivity assumptions. That is, wage increases in both sectors are identical. Wage increases in the non-health sector are more than covered by productivity increases, thus allowing the price remain constant over time. Since productivity is stagnant in the health sector, prices must rise over time to cover the difference between low labor productivity and increasing wages, as discussed in section 6.1.

We arbitrarily set a price of 5 for the non-health sector and an initial price of 8 in the health sector for both countries.

5) *Labor Force Allocation Between Sectors:* The initial allocation of the labor force between the two sectors is set by the percentages of the population employed in the health sector and of those over 65 as of 1990. This information is easily supported in OECD labor data. The remaining portion is said to be employed in the non-health sector. In Japan the labor allocation breakdown is 82 in non-health and 6 in the health sector. In the U.S. this breakdown is 76.9 non-health and 10.49 in health.

Over the course of the time period studied, this allocation is determined by the aging ratio, and the ratio of output in the two sectors. We assume a constant ratio of output in the non-health sector to the health sector. We then derive a bernoulli-type differential equation to determine the allocation of labor between sectors over time. The appendix explains this in detail.

6) *Health Care Expenditures Ratio to GDP:* Table 9 reports that ratios of health care expenditures to GDP were 6.44 percent for Japan and 12.08 percent for the U.S. in 1990. In our simulations we use these two statistics as a base for deriving the market value of per capita output in both sectors (y_1 and y_2) and thus per capita GDP. These are derived in consistency with the other assumptions such as productivity. They are not to be compared to the aggregate GDP in Japan or the U.S. We start with the derived figures as given in 1990 and allow the model to determine the changes of this ratio over time. Our model has the health care expenditures to GDP determined endogenously based on the calcu-

lation of both the market value of health care output (y_2) and the market value of the total output (y) for each country.

7) We also include the elasticity of health services which measures the ratio of the growth of health expenditures $\frac{\dot{y_2}}{y_2}$ to the growth in GDP $\frac{\dot{y}}{y}$. This statistic gives a good indication of how fast the health sector is expanding in terms of the gross economy. This is not the same as income elasticity which is derived in Appendix B.

8) Total GDP for each country is equal to the sum of market values of output in the two sectors of the economy. The output is calculated per capita and hence GDP is calculated per capita. In our simulations per capita GDP begins at 900.00 for the U.S. and 880.00 for Japan in 1990. The table below gives the first period derivation of GDP, or y_0, for both countries.

Japan

Sector	l_0	D_0	q_0	P_0	y_0
Non-health	82.00	2.00	164.00	5.00	820.00
Health	6.00	1.25	7.50	8.00	60.00
					880.00

The U.S.

Sector	l_0	D_0	q_0	P_0	y_0
Non-health	76.90	2.06	158.40	5.00	792.00
Health	10.50	1.29	13.50	8.00	108.00
					900.00

CHAPTER 8

SIMULATION RESULTS

Using the assumptions and initial conditions discussed in Chapter 7, we simulated two cases for Japan and two for the U.S. using two different labor productivity growth rates for each country and two different labor productivity growth rates for the health sector for each country. The first two simulations refer to Japan while the last two refer to the U.S. In the first simulation for Japan, we set the labor productivity growth rate for the non-health sector at 3 percent and that for the health sector at 1 percent. In simulation 2, these labor productivity growth rates are set at 3 percent and 0 percent respectively. For the U.S. in simulation 3, we set the labor productivity growth rate for the non-health sector at 2 percent and that for the health sector at 0 percent. For simulation 4, these rates are 2 percent and 0 percent respectively. These growth rates are based on recent empirical studies.[98]

The most notable variables explored are inflation in both the health sector and the whole economy. In particular, we show how inflation in the health sector rises considerably faster than the economy as a whole. All four of the simulations, however, have diminishing rate of inflation in both the health sector and the economy due to the concavity in the flow of labor from the non-health sector into the health sector. A table for each simulation is provided along with a reduced table showing growth rates of wages, labor and the market value of output for health and the whole economy. This table is to show the change in growth from the first few periods to the last few periods.

Since productivity in the non-health sector is rising, labor exits this sector to retire *and* to move into the health sector. Labor in the non-health sector is declining at an increasing rate, but at a significantly slower rate than productivity growth, while labor in the health sector grows at a declining rate. This concavity in the growth of health expenditures ($\frac{\dot{y_2}}{y_2}$), the growth rate of GDP ($\frac{\dot{y}}{y}$), frequently referred to as inflation and the growth rate of labor in the health sector is an issue we recognize but do not explore in great detail. It is simply a by-product of the model which is explained in greater detail in the appendix.

Throughout the simulations we will be discussing both price changes and inflation. The prices, or relative prices, (P_1/P_2) grow at a constant rate depending on the given parameters per simulation. That is, the price ratio grows at a rate that equals the difference in the productivity growth rates $(\gamma_1 - \gamma_2)$. This is explained in the appendix. The growth rate of the market value of output ($\frac{\dot{y}_i}{y_i}$ for $i = 1, 2$) as we mentioned does not grow at a steady rate. We also discuss the elasticity of health services which simply measures the growth in the health sector to the growth in GDP ($\frac{\dot{y}_2/y_2}{\dot{y}/y}$). In many simulations, this statistic is quite smooth implying that the health sector grows in proportion to the GDP, but in no simulation is the elasticity constant.

In order to derive the rate of transfer of labor from the productivity-leading sector to the productivity-lagging sector, we establish the assumption that the ratio of output in the productivity-leading sector to that in the productivity-lagging sector is constant (q_1/q_2). Since there is no savings and no inventory in this model, all that is produced is consumed. Given a non-additive concave utility function, we are able to derive the indifference curves and income expansion path of the two goods. The time path of the production transformation curve as well as the income expansion path reveals that preferences are non-homothetic. This is shown in figures 1-3. This assumption concerning (q_1/q_2) allows us to derive a differential equation for l_1 and l_2, the relative labor ratios. Appendix II solves for an income elasticity of health care greater than one, which is consistent with the non-homothetic preferences. In addition, the production transformation curve is linear due to homogeneity of labor that implies that at any level of output, the rate of transforming production away from one good to produce the other is constant and equals the ratio of productivity measures. This is based on a linear production function for both goods that is maintained in every simulation.

We are focusing on health care expenditures. Expenditures in the non-health sector implies the market value of goods, $[P_1 \cdot q_1 = y_1]$, the price of the non-health sector remains the same. Thus, q_1 and y_1 are rising at equal rates over time.

Finally, the continuous transfer of resources from one sector of the economy to the other does not drain the productive part of the economy at a constant level. Even though the society is aging at a constant rate, those employed in the non-health sector will continue to increase output in their sector. Thus, in keeping with a constant ration of q_1/q_2, q_1 and q_2 rise at the same rate over time.

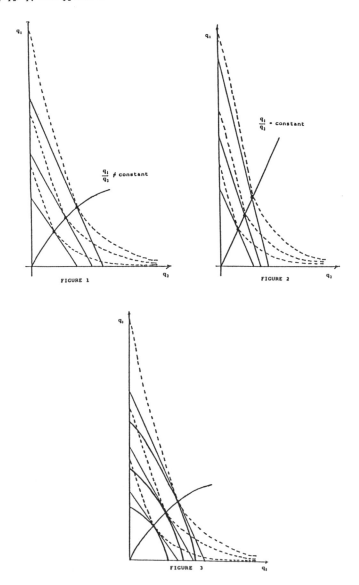

FIGURE 1

FIGURE 2

FIGURE 3

Table S1 - Simulation 1 (Japan: $\gamma_1 = 3\%$, $\gamma_2 = 1\%$)

Year	Wage	Non-Health					Health					Retired	
		D_1	P_1	L_1/N	Q_1/N	Y_1/N	D_2	P_2	L_2/N	Q_2/N	Y_2/N	L_r/N	q_1/q_2
1990	10.00	2.00	5	82.00	164.00	820.00	1.25	8.00	6.00	7.50	60.00	11.90	22
1991	10.30	2.06	5	81.77	168.44	842.18	1.26	8.16	6.10	7.70	62.86	12.13	22
1992	10.61	2.12	5	81.43	172.78	863.91	1.28	8.32	6.20	7.90	65.77	12.37	22
1993	10.93	2.19	5	81.09	177.23	886.13	1.29	8.49	6.30	8.11	68.81	12.61	22
1994	11.26	2.25	5	80.75	181.77	908.83	1.30	8.66	6.40	8.32	71.98	12.86	22
1995	11.59	2.32	5	80.40	186.41	932.03	1.31	8.83	6.50	8.53	75.30	13.11	22
1996	11.94	2.39	5	80.04	191.15	955.74	1.33	9.01	6.60	8.75	78.76	13.36	22
1997	12.30	2.46	5	79.68	195.99	979.96	1.34	9.19	6.70	8.98	82.37	13.62	22
1998	12.67	2.53	5	79.31	200.94	1004.69	1.35	9.37	6.80	9.20	86.13	13.89	22
1999	13.05	2.61	5	78.94	205.99	1029.95	1.37	9.56	6.90	9.44	90.07	14.16	22
2000	13.44	2.69	5	78.56	211.15	1055.74	1.38	9.75	7.01	9.67	94.17	14.44	22
2001	13.84	2.77	5	78.17	216.41	1082.06	1.39	9.95	7.11	9.92	98.44	14.72	22
2002	14.26	2.85	5	77.78	221.78	1108.92	1.41	10.15	7.22	10.17	102.91	15.00	22
2003	14.69	2.94	5	77.38	227.27	1136.33	1.42	10.35	7.32	10.42	107.56	15.30	22
2004	15.13	3.03	5	76.97	232.86	1164.28	1.44	10.56	7.43	10.68	112.41	15.60	22
2005	15.58	3.12	5	76.56	238.56	1192.78	1.45	10.77	7.54	10.94	117.46	15.90	22
2006	16.05	3.21	5	76.14	244.37	1221.84	1.47	10.98	7.65	11.21	122.73	16.21	22
2007	16.53	3.31	5	75.72	250.29	1251.47	1.48	11.20	7.76	11.48	128.22	16.53	22
2008	17.02	3.40	5	75.28	256.33	1281.65	1.50	11.43	7.87	11.76	133.94	16.85	22
2009	17.54	3.51	5	74.84	262.48	1312.40	1.51	11.65	7.98	12.05	139.90	17.18	22
2010	18.06	3.61	5	74.40	268.74	1343.71	1.53	11.89	8.09	12.34	146.10	17.51	22

Table S1 - Simulation 1 (Japan: $\gamma_1 = 3\%$, $\gamma_2 = 1\%$) (cont'd)

Year	Wage	Non-Health					Health					Retired	
		D_1	P_1	L_1/N	Q_1/N	Y_1/N	D_2	P_2	L_2/N	Q_2/N	Y_2/N	L_r/N	q_1/q_2
2011	18.60	3.72	5	73.94	275.12	1375.59	1.54	12.13	8.20	12.63	152.56	17.85	22
2012	19.16	3.83	5	73.48	281.61	1408.04	1.56	12.37	8.31	12.93	159.28	18.20	22
2013	19.74	3.95	5	73.02	288.21	1441.06	1.57	12.62	8.42	13.24	166.27	18.56	22
2014	20.33	4.07	5	72.54	294.93	1747.64	1.59	12.87	8.54	13.55	173.55	18.92	22
2015	20.94	4.19	5	72.06	301.76	1508.79	1.60	13.12	8.65	13.87	181.12	19.29	22
2016	21.57	4.31	5	71.57	308.70	1543.50	1.62	13.39	8.76	14.19	188.99	19.67	22
2017	22.21	4.44	5	71.07	315.75	1578.77	1.64	13.66	8.88	14.52	197.18	20.05	22
2018	22.88	4.58	5	70.57	322.92	1614.59	1.65	13.93	8.99	14.85	205.69	20.44	22
2019	23.57	4.71	5	70.06	330.19	1650.96	1.67	14.21	9.10	15.19	214.53	20.84	22
2020	24.27	4.85	5	69.54	337.57	1687.87	1.68	14.49	9.22	15.53	223.71	21.25	22
2021	25.00	5.00	5	69.01	345.06	1725.32	1.70	14.78	9.33	15.88	233.25	21.66	22
2022	25.75	5.15	5	68.48	352.66	1763.30	1.72	15.08	9.44	16.23	243.15	22.08	22
2023	26.52	5.30	5	67.93	360.36	1801.79	1.74	15.38	9.55	16.59	253.42	22.51	22
2024	27.32	5.46	5	67.38	368.16	1840.78	1.75	15.69	9.67	16.95	264.09	22.95	22
2025	28.14	5.63	5	66.82	376.05	1880.27	1.77	16.00	9.78	17.31	275.15	23.40	22

Note: $D_1(t) = 1.03 * D_1(t-1)$
$D_2(t) = 1.01 * D_2(t-1)$

Table S2 - Simulation 2 (Japan: $\gamma_1 = 3\%$, $\gamma_2 = 0\%$)

Year	Wage	Non-Health					Health					Retired	
		D_1	P_1	L_1/N	Q_1/N	Y_1/N	D_2	P_2	L_2/N	Q_2/N	Y_2/N	L_r/N	q_1/q_2
1990	10.00	2.00	5	82.00	164.00	820.00	1.25	8.00	6.00	7.50	60.00	11.90	22
1991	10.30	2.06	5	81.71	168.32	841.61	1.25	8.24	6.16	7.70	63.43	12.13	22
1992	10.61	2.12	5	81.32	172.54	862.71	1.25	8.49	6.31	7.89	66.97	12.37	22
1993	10.93	2.19	5	80.92	176.85	884.23	1.25	8.74	6.47	8.09	70.70	12.61	22
1994	11.26	2.25	5	80.51	181.24	906.18	1.25	9.00	6.63	8.29	74.63	12.86	22
1995	11.59	2.32	5	80.10	185.71	928.56	1.25	9.27	6.79	8.49	78.77	13.11	22
1996	11.94	2.39	5	79.68	190.27	951.37	1.25	9.55	6.96	8.70	83.12	13.36	22
1997	12.30	2.46	5	79.25	194.92	974.62	1.25	9.84	7.13	8.91	87.71	13.62	22
1998	12.67	2.53	5	78.81	199.66	998.30	1.25	10.13	7.30	9.13	92.53	13.89	22
1999	13.05	2.61	5	78.36	204.48	1022.41	1.25	10.44	7.48	9.35	97.61	14.16	22
2000	13.44	2.69	5	77.90	209.39	1046.95	1.25	10.75	7.66	9.58	102.95	14.44	22
2001	13.84	2.77	5	77.44	214.39	1071.93	1.25	11.07	7.84	9.80	108.57	14.72	22
2002	14.26	2.85	5	76.97	219.47	1097.35	1.25	11.41	8.03	10.04	114.48	15.00	22
2003	14.69	2.94	5	76.48	224.64	1123.19	1.25	11.75	8.22	10.27	120.69	15.30	22
2004	15.13	3.03	5	75.99	229.89	1149.47	1.25	12.10	8.41	10.51	127.22	15.60	22
2005	15.58	3.12	5	75.49	235.23	1176.17	1.25	12.46	8.61	10.76	134.08	15.90	22
2006	16.05	3.21	5	74.98	240.66	1203.29	1.25	12.84	8.80	11.01	141.29	16.21	22
2007	16.53	3.31	5	74.47	246.17	1230.83	1.25	13.22	9.01	11.26	148.86	16.53	22
2008	17.02	3.40	5	73.94	251.76	1258.78	1.25	13.62	9.21	11.51	156.80	16.85	22
2009	17.54	3.51	5	73.40	257.43	1287.14	1.25	14.03	9.42	11.77	165.15	17.18	22
2010	18.06	3.61	5	72.86	263.18	1315.91	1.25	14.45	9.63	12.04	173.90	17.51	22

Table S2 - Simulation 2 (Japan: $\gamma_1 = 3\%$, $\gamma_2 = 0\%$)　(cont'd)

Year	Wage	Non-Health					Health					Retired	
		D_1	P_1	L_1/N	Q_1/N	Y_1/N	D_2	P_2	L_2/N	Q_2/N	Y_2/N	L_r/N	q_1/q_2
2011	18.60	3.72	5	72.30	269.01	1345.06	1.25	14.88	9.84	12.30	213.41	18.92	22
2012	19.16	3.83	5	71.74	274.92	1374.60	1.25	15.33	10.06	12.57	224.50	19.29	22
2013	19.74	3.95	5	71.17	280.90	1404.51	1.25	15.79	10.28	12.85	236.13	19.67	22
2017	22.21	4.44	5	68.77	305.53	1527.65	1.25	17.77	11.18	13.97	248.29	20.05	22
2018	22.88	4.58	5	68.15	311.85	1559.24	1.25	18.30	11.41	14.26	261.03	20.44	22
2019	23.57	4.71	5	67.52	318.23	1591.13	1.25	18.85	11.64	14.55	274.36	20.84	22
2020	24.27	4.85	5	66.88	324.66	1623.28	1.25	19.42	11.88	14.85	288.30	21.25	22
2021	25.00	5.00	5	66.23	331.14	1655.69	1.25	20.00	12.11	15.14	302.88	21.66	22
2022	25.75	5.15	5	65.56	337.67	1688.33	1.25	20.60	12.35	15.44	318.12	22.08	22
2023	26.52	5.30	5	64.89	344.24	1721.18	1.25	21.22	12.59	15.74	334.03	22.51	22
2024	27.32	5.46	5	64.21	350.84	1754.21	1.25	21.86	12.84	16.04	350.66	22.95	22
2025	28.14	5.63	5	63.52	357.48	1787.41	1.25	22.51	13.08	16.35	368.01	23.40	22

Note: $D_1(t) = 1.03 * D_1(t-1)$
　　　$D_2(t) = 1.00 * D_2(t-1)$

Table S3 - Simulation 3 (The United States: $\gamma_1 = 2\%$, $\gamma_2 = 1\%$)

Year	Wage	D_1	P_1	Non-Health			D_2	P_2	Health			Retired	q_1/q_2
				L_1/N	Q_1/N	Y_1/N			L_2/N	Q_2/N	Y_2/N	L_r/N	
1990	10.00	2.06	5	76.91	158.40	792.00	1.29	8.00	10.49	13.50	108.00	12.60	12
1991	10.51	2.10	5	76.71	161.18	805.88	1.30	8.08	10.57	13.77	111.02	12.73	12
1992	10.72	2.14	5	76.50	163.96	819.81	1.32	8.16	10.64	14.01	114.06	12.85	12
1993	10.93	2.19	5	76.30	166.79	833.96	1.33	8.24	10.72	14.25	117.19	12.98	12
1994	11.15	2.23	5	76.09	169.66	848.32	1.34	8.32	10.80	14.50	120.40	13.11	12
1995	11.37	2.27	5	75.88	172.58	862.91	1.36	8.41	10.88	14.75	123.70	13.24	12
1996	11.60	2.32	5	75.67	175.54	877.72	1.37	8.49	10.96	15.00	127.08	13.38	12
1997	11.83	2.37	5	75.46	178.55	892.77	1.38	8.58	11.03	15.26	130.55	13.51	12
1998	12.07	2.41	5	75.24	181.61	908.04	1.40	8.66	11.11	15.52	134.11	13.64	12
1999	12.31	2.46	5	75.03	184.71	923.55	1.41	8.75	11.19	15.79	137.77	13.78	12
2000	12.56	2.51	5	74.81	187.86	939.29	1.42	8.84	11.27	16.06	141.52	13.92	12
2001	12.81	2.56	5	74.59	191.06	955.28	1.44	8.93	11.35	16.34	145.36	14.06	12
2002	13.06	2.61	5	74.37	194.30	971.51	1.45	9.01	11.43	16.62	149.31	14.20	12
2003	13.32	2.66	5	74.15	197.60	987.98	1.47	9.10	11.51	16.90	153.36	14.34	12
2004	13.59	2.72	5	73.93	200.94	1004.71	1.48	9.20	11.59	17.19	157.52	14.48	12
2005	13.86	2.77	5	73.70	204.34	1021.68	1.50	9.29	11.67	17.48	161.78	14.63	12
2006	14.14	2.83	5	73.47	207.78	1038.91	1.51	9.38	11.75	17.77	166.15	14.77	12
2007	14.42	2.88	5	73.25	211.28	1056.39	1.53	9.47	11.83	18.08	170.64	14.92	12
2008	14.71	2.94	5	73.02	214.83	1074.14	1.54	9.57	11.91	18.38	175.24	15.07	12
2009	15.01	3.00	5	72.78	218.43	1092.14	1.56	9.66	11.99	18.69	179.96	15.22	12
2010	15.31	3.06	5	72.55	222.08	1110.42	1.57	9.76	12.07	19.01	184.80	15.37	12

Table S3 - Simulation 3 (The United States: $\gamma_1 = 2\%$, $\gamma_2 = 1\%$) (cont'd)

Year	Wage	Non-health					Health					Retired	
		D_1	P_1	L_1/N	Q_1/N	Y_1/N	D_2	P_2	L_2/N	Q_2/N	Y_2/N	L_r/N	q_1/q_2
2011	15.61	3.12	5	72.32	225.79	1128.96	1.59	9.86	12.16	19.32	189.77	15.53	12
2012	15.92	3.18	5	72.08	229.55	1147.77	1.61	9.96	12.24	19.65	194.86	15.68	12
2013	16.24	3.25	5	71.84	233.37	1166.85	1.62	10.06	12.32	19.98	200.08	15.84	12
2014	16.57	3.31	5	71.60	237.24	1186.21	1.64	10.16	12.40	20.31	205.43	16.00	12
2015	16.90	3.38	5	71.36	241.17	1205.85	1.65	10.26	12.48	20.65	210.92	16.16	12
2016	17.24	3.45	5	71.12	245.15	1225.77	1.67	10.36	12.56	20.99	216.55	16.32	12
2017	17.58	3.52	5	70.87	249.20	1245.98	1.69	10.47	12.65	21.34	222.32	16.48	12
2018	17.93	3.59	5	70.62	253.29	1266.47	1.70	10.57	12.73	21.69	228.24	16.65	12
2019	18.29	3.66	5	70.38	257.45	1287.26	1.72	10.68	12.81	22.05	234.30	16.81	12
2020	18.66	3.73	5	70.13	261.67	1308.33	1.74	10.78	12.89	22.42	240.52	16.98	12
2021	19.03	3.81	5	69.87	265.94	1329.70	1.76	10.89	12.97	22.78	246.89	17.15	12
2022	19.41	3.88	5	69.62	270.27	1351.37	1.77	11.00	13.06	23.16	253.43	17.32	12
2023	19.80	3.96	5	69.36	274.67	1373.34	1.79	11.11	13.14	23.54	260.12	17.50	12
2024	20.19	4.04	5	69.11	279.12	1395.62	1.81	11.22	13.22	23.92	266.98	17.67	12
2025	20.60	4.12	5	68.85	283.64	1418.20	1.83	11.33	13.30	24.31	274.02	17.85	12

Note: $D_1(t) = 1.02 * D_1(t-1)$
$D_2(t) = 1.01 * D_2(t-1)$

Table S4 - Simulation 4 (The United States: $\gamma_1 = 2$, $\gamma_2 = 0\%$)

Year	Wage	Non-Health					Health					Retired	
		D_1	P_1	L_1/N	Q_1/N	Y_1/N	D_2	P_2	L_2/N	Q_2/N	Y_2/N	L_r/N	q_1/q_2
1990	10.30	2.06	5	76.91	158.40	792.00	1.29	8.00	10.49	13.50	108.00	12.60	12
1991	10.51	2.10	5	76.62	160.98	804.92	1.29	8.16	10.66	13.75	111.98	12.73	12
1992	10.72	2.14	5	76.32	163.56	817.82	1.29	8.32	10.83	13.97	116.05	12.85	12
1993	10.93	2.19	5	76.02	166.18	830.88	1.29	8.49	11.00	14.19	120.26	12.98	12
1994	11.15	2.23	5	75.71	168.82	844.10	1.29	8.66	11.18	14.42	124.62	13.11	12
1995	11.37	2.27	5	75.40	171.50	857.48	1.29	8.83	11.35	14.65	129.13	13.24	12
1996	11.60	2.32	5	75.09	174.20	871.01	1.29	9.01	11.53	14.88	133.79	13.38	12
1997	11.83	2.37	5	74.78	176.94	884.71	1.29	9.19	11.72	15.11	138.61	13.51	12
1998	12.07	2.41	5	74.46	179.71	898.56	1.29	9.37	11.90	15.35	143.60	13.64	12
1999	12.31	2.46	5	74.14	182.51	912.57	1.29	9.56	12.08	15.59	148.75	13.78	12
2000	12.56	2.51	5	73.81	185.35	926.73	1.29	9.75	12.27	15.83	154.08	13.92	12
2001	12.81	2.56	5	73.48	188.21	941.05	1.29	9.95	12.46	16.08	159.59	14.06	12
2002	13.06	2.61	5	73.15	191.11	955.53	1.29	10.15	12.65	16.32	165.29	14.20	12
2003	13.32	2.66	5	72.81	194.03	970.17	1.29	10.35	12.85	16.57	171.18	14.34	12
2004	13.59	2.72	5	72.47	196.99	984.96	1.29	10.56	13.04	16.83	177.26	14.48	12
2005	13.86	2.77	5	72.13	199.98	999.91	1.29	10.77	13.24	17.08	183.55	14.63	12
2006	14.14	2.83	5	71.78	203.00	1015.01	1.29	10.98	13.44	17.34	190.05	14.77	12
2007	14.42	2.88	5	71.43	206.05	1030.27	1.29	11.20	13.64	17.60	196.76	14.92	12
2008	14.71	2.94	5	71.08	209.14	1045.68	1.29	11.43	13.85	17.86	203.70	15.07	12
2009	15.01	3.00	5	70.72	212.25	1061.24	1.29	11.65	14.05	18.13	210.87	15.22	12
2010	15.31	3.06	5	70.36	215.39	1076.95	1.29	11.89	14.26	18.40	218.27	15.37	12

Table S4 - Simulation 4 (The United States: $\gamma_1 = 2$, $\gamma_2 = 0\%$) (cont'd)

| Year | Wage | Non-Health | | | | | | Health | | | | | | Retired | |
		D_1	P_1	L_1/N	Q_1/N	Y_1/N	D_2	P_2	L_2/N	Q_2/N	Y_2/N	L_r/N	q_1/q_2
2011	15.61	3.12	5	70.00	218.56	1092.81	1.29	12.13	14.47	18.67	225.91	15.53	12
2012	15.92	3.18	5	69.63	221.76	1108.82	1.29	12.37	14.68	18.94	233.81	15.68	12
2013	16.24	3.25	5	69.26	224.99	1124.97	1.29	12.62	14.90	19.22	241.96	15.84	12
2014	16.57	3.31	5	68.89	228.25	1141.27	1.29	12.87	15.11	19.50	250.37	16.00	12
2015	16.90	3.38	5	68.51	231.54	1157.71	1.29	13.12	15.33	19.78	259.06	16.16	12
2016	17.24	3.45	5	68.13	234.86	1174.30	1.29	13.39	15.55	20.06	268.02	16.32	12
2017	17.58	3.52	5	67.75	238.20	1191.02	1.29	13.66	15.77	20.35	277.28	16.48	12
2018	17.93	3.59	5	67.36	241.58	1207.88	1.29	13.93	15.99	20.63	286.83	16.65	12
2019	18.29	3.66	5	66.97	244.98	1224.88	1.29	14.21	16.22	20.92	296.68	16.81	12
2020	18.66	3.73	5	66.57	248.40	1242.01	1.29	14.49	16.45	21.22	306.85	16.98	12
2021	19.03	3.81	5	66.17	251.85	1259.26	1.29	14.78	16.68	21.51	317.33	17.15	12
2022	19.41	3.88	5	65.77	255.33	1276.65	1.29	15.08	16.91	21.81	328.15	17.32	12
2023	19.80	3.96	5	65.37	258.83	1294.16	1.29	15.38	17.14	22.11	339.30	17.50	12
2024	20.91	4.04	5	64.96	262.36	1311.80	1.29	15.69	17.37	22.41	350.80	17.67	12
2025	20.60	4.12	5	64.54	265.91	1329.55	1.29	16.00	17.61	22.71	362.66	17.85	12

Note: $D_1(t) = 1.02*D_1(t-1)$
$D_2(t) = 1.00*D_2(t-1)$

8.1 The Japanese Case Simulation 1

1) A 3 percent productivity growth rate for the non-health sector and a 1 percent productivity growth rate for health care output will double the relative price of the health sector (P_2/P_1) in 35 years from 8 to 16. Recall that the price of output from the non-health sector, P_1, remains stable at 5 over time. It is shown in the appendix that the growth rate in the relative price is equal to the difference in the two growth rates of productivity. In this case this difference is 3% - 1% = 2%. The relative price measures the price paid for the same service in different years.

2) More importantly, inflation in the health sector which measures the rate of growth of y_2 starts out at 4.8 percent but slows down to 4.2 percent by 2025, while inflation for the economy (GDP) starts at 2.9 percent and ends at 2.4 percent. This is quite reflective of the true scenario in today's economy; that is, costs in healthcare have risen at a substantially faster pace than inflation. This simulation shows that this trend is endemic to the economy, and there is no reason to believe it will not continue into the future.

3) The wage rate (W) is the same in both sectors, as was discussed, and it grows at the same rate as productivity in the non-health sector (3 percent in this case). As a result, the wage rate starting at 10.00, doubles in 24 years and reaches 28.14 in the year 2025. It is interesting to observe that since inflation slows over time, at the start of this simulation, wages rise at a relatively similar pace as inflation. But in time, wages rise at a faster rate than inflation.

This is linked to the income elasticity for health care which in our simulations is greater than one. In other words, as income rises (wages), we spend a greater portion of the higher income on health services, and a lower portion on other goods. Thus, even though wages rise faster than inflation, their rises are lower than inflation in health care. We discuss this issue in greater detail in appendix B. Nevertheless, even with non-homothetic preferences, the ratio of output q_1/q_2 is constant overtime (See above).

4) The labor force as a percentage of the population declines from 88 percent in 1990 [82 percent for non-health sector and 6 percent for the health sector] to 76.6 percent in 2025 [66.82 percent for non-health sector and 9.8 percent for the health sector]. This decline is a result of the aging population during the 35 year period which is increasing at the constant rate of 1.95 percent per annum. Specifically, labor in health initially rises at a rate of 1.67 percent and then

slows to a growth rate of 1.14 percent, while labor in the non-health sector declines at a rate of 0.28 percent at the start of the model and declines faster at a rate of 0.83 percent by 2025.

Although the labor force as a percentage of the population declines over the time period studied, the output in both sectors is growing due to increased productivity in the non-health sector. This, coupled with the constant transfer of labor resources to the health sector, increases the output in the health sector as well. This positive growth rate in GDP with a shrinking labor force seems untenable. It not only is feasible, it has been sustained over the past several years.[98] Continued growth in productivity will ensure future growth rates in GDP in an aging society.

5) The ratio of health care expenditures to GDP is rising. It is initially 6.8 percent, which is in line with the literature and by 2025 climbs to a rate of 12.8. The increase in this ratio is a result of the increasing health care cost brought on by an increasing per unit of output labor cost as well as higher demand from the aging population. It is this variable that concerns most economists and officials. The income elasticity of health services, which is not the same as the growth rate of this ratio, starts at 1.68 and then progresses to a growth rate of 1.74. This relatively slow growth is in line with historic statistics and demonstrates our point in this study. Indeed, Japan's economy will be committing more and more resources towards health services, particularly for the elderly, and these services will comprise a greater share of the GDP, but as long as the remainder of the economy maintains consistent productivity growth, this greater demand for health services can be financed by the economy.

Table S1A below lists the labor, output, market value of output in the health sector and GDP along with their respective growth rates and the elasticity of health services to GDP for the first and last four years of the time period studied.

Table S1A

Japan: $\gamma_1 = 3\%$, $\gamma_2 = 1\%$

Year	l_2	$\dfrac{\dot{l_2}}{l_2}$ (%)	q_2	$\dfrac{\dot{q_2}}{q_2}$ (%)	y_2	$\dfrac{\dot{y_2}}{y_2}$ (%)	y	$\dfrac{\dot{y}}{y}$ (%)	Income Elasticity (%)
1990	6.00		7.50		60.00		880.00		
1991	6.10	1.67	7.70	2.67	62.86	4.77	905.04	2.85	1.68
1992	6.20	1.64	7.90	2.60	65.77	4.63	929.68	2.72	1.70
1993	6.30	1.61	8.11	2.66	68.81	4.62	954.94	2.72	1.70
2022	9.44	1.18	16.23	2.20	243.15	4.24	2006.45	2.44	1.74
2023	9.55	1.17	16.59	2.22	253.42	4.22	2055.21	2.43	1.74
2024	9.67	1.26	16.95	2.17	264.09	4.21	2104.87	2.42	1.74
2025	9.78	1.14	17.31	2.12	275.15	4.19	2155.42	2.40	1.74

8.2 The Japanese Case Simulation 2

In this simulation the growth rates of GDP is the same as that in simulation 1. This may seem unfeasible at first, but is consistent with the constant ratio of q_1/q_2 which is also the same as in simulation 1.

1) A 3 percent productivity growth rate for the non-health sector and a 0 percent productivity growth rate for health care output will double the relative price of the health sector (P_2/P_1) in 24 years from 8 to 16 and will cause the price to reach 22.5 by the year 2025. Since the relative price growth equals the difference in the two growth rates of productivity, the price of health services rises at a rate of 3 percent: (3% - 0%).

2) Inflation in the health sector, the rate of growth of y_2 starts out at 5.72 percent but slows down to 4.95 percent by 2025, while inflation for the economy (GDP) is the same as in simulation 1, it starts at 2.9 percent and ends at 2.4 percent. The inflation in the health sector is most dramatic in this scenario, and it represents the more pronounced difference in productivity. A productivity growth rate of 0 in the health sector translates into higher labor costs per unit of output which are then passed on to the consumer via higher prices.

3) The wage rate (W) is the same in both sectors, as was discussed, and it grows at the same rate as productivity in the non-health sector (3 percent in this case). This result is the same as in simulation 1.

4) The labor force as a percentage of the population declines at the same pace as in simulation 1, since the growth rate of the aging ratio has not changed. However, with a 0 growth rate of productivity in the health sector, labor resources must be transferred from the non-health to the health sector at a faster pace. This is explained in the appendix and in section above that shows that the transfer rate of labor from one sector to the other is a function of the two productivity growth rates, based on the premise of holding the ratio of q_1/q_2 constant. Thus, in 1990, 82 percent of the population is in the non-health sector and 6 is in the health sector, by 2025, 63.5 percent of the population is in the non-health sector and 13.08 percent is in the stagnant sector. This represents more than twice as many in health services in 2025 than there is today. More specifically, labor in health initially rises at a rate of 2.67 percent and then slows to a growth rate of 1.87 percent, while labor in the non-health sector declines at a rate of 0.35 percent at the start of the model and declines faster at a rate of 1.07 percent by 2025.

5) The ratio of health care expenditures to GDP is rising. It is initially 6.8 percent, in line with the literature and by 2025 climbs to a rate of 17.1 percent versus 12.8 percent in simulation 1. The elasticity is declining from 2.01 in 1991 to 2.06 in 2025. Nevertheless, the percentage of GDP going toward health services is rising faster in this simulation without productivity growth in the health sector than when the economy enjoys some productivity gains in health as in simulation 1. The higher growth in elasticity is a result of the productivity differences that exacerbate the per unit of output labor costs in health services and hence the economy's allocation of resources. In other words, even though GDP is the same in simulation 2 as in simulation 1, the health sector makes up a greater share of GDP in time when the industry has no productivity growth. The difference in elasticity, however, is less than one-half of a point.

Table S2A below lists the labor, output, market value of output in the health sector and GDP along with their respective growth rates and the elasticity of health services to GDP for the first and last four years of the time period studied.

Table S2A

Japan: $\gamma_1 = 3\%$, $\gamma_2 = 0\%$

Year	l_2	$\dfrac{\dot{l_2}}{l_2}$ (%)	q_2	$\dfrac{\dot{q_2}}{q_2}$ (%)	y_2	$\dfrac{\dot{y_2}}{y_2}$ (%)	y	$\dfrac{\dot{y}}{y}$ (%)	Income Elasticity (%)
1990	6.00		7.50		60.00		880.00		
1991	6.16	2.67	7.70	2.67	63.43	5.72	905.04	2.85	2.01
1992	6.31	2.44	7.89	2.47	66.97	5.58	929.68	2.72	2.05
1993	6.47	2.54	8.09	2.53	70.70	5.57	954.94	2.72	2.05
2022	12.35	1.98	15.44	1.98	318.12	5.03	2006.45	2.44	2.06
2023	12.59	1.94	15.74	1.94	334.03	5.00	2055.21	2.43	2.06
2024	12.84	1.99	16.04	1.91	350.66	4.98	2104.87	2.42	2.06
2025	13.08	1.87	16.35	1.93	368.01	4.95	2155.42	2.40	2.06

Again, the continuous transfer of resources form one sector of the economy to the other does not drain the productive part of the economy at a constant level but it appears to do so more in this simulation than in the last. Even though the labor is transferred more rapidly, those employed in the non-health sector will continue to increase output in their sector.

8.3 The United States Case Simulation 3

The simulations for the United States follow the same assumptions as those used in the simulations for Japan, except for different growth rates for the elderly, different growth rates for productivity in the productivity-progressive sector, and different initial conditions. In maintaining a consistency in output that is in line with the Untied States' initial conditions, we held the ratio of output in the two sectors (q_1/q_2) constant at a rate of 12 versus 22 in Japan. This appears to be a significant difference in that the ratio of productive output to non-productive output (health) in Japan is close to twice as much as that in the United States. This is balanced, however, by a difference in the growth rate of health care expenditures to GDP as will be shown in number 5.

In this simulation, the growth rates of the productive sector is 2 percent, while the growth rate in the non-health sector is 1 percent. The growth rate of the aged ratio is 1 percent.

1) A 2 percent productivity growth rate for the non-health sector and a 1 percent productivity growth rate for health care output will cause the relative price of the health sector (P_2/P_1) to climb from 8 to 11.33 by the year 2025. Since the relative price growth equals the difference in the two growth rates of productivity, the price of health services rises at a rate of 1 percent: (2% - 1 %). This is considerably less than the price increase for Japan. As a consequence of a low productivity growth rate for the United States' productivity-progressive sector in this simulation, the growth rate of labor costs is less severe. This is more evident in the discussion of wages below.

2) Inflation in the health sector, the rate of growth of y_2 starts out at 2.8 percent and slows to 2.6 percent while inflation in the total economy (GDP) is 1.9 percent at the start of the period studied and then slows slightly to 1.8 percent. This may appear low to many, especially those Americans who have seen their health bills rise at much higher rates. In running the simulations we generated many possible scenarios. In this simulation, we simply argue that given the initial parameters that include a productivity growth rate of 2 percent in the progressive sector and a 1 percent growth rate of productivity in the stagnant sector, inflation is lower.

3) The wage rate (W) is the same in both sectors, as was discussed, and it grows at the same rate a productivity in the non-health sector (2 percent in this case). As a result the wage rate starting at 10.30, doubles in the 35 years studied until 2025. In this simulation, wages are rising slightly faster than inflation, but slower than the inflation in health services. As discussed in simulation 1, this is consistent with the income elasticity greater than one, or as incomes rise, we spend a higher portion of income on health services.

4) The labor force as a percentage of the population declines from 87.4 percent in 1990 [76.9 percent for non-health sector and 10.5 percent for the health sector] to 83.2 percent in 2025 [68.9 percent for non-health sector and 13.3 percent for the health sector] This decline is a result of the aging population during the 35 year period which is increasing at the constant rate of 1.01 percent per annum. Specifically, labor in health initially rises at a rate of 0.7 percent and slows to a growth rate of 0.6 percent. As discussed, this slow growth rate is also a function of the different growth rates of productivity in the economy.

5) The ratio of health care expenditures to GDP is rising in this simulation as well. It is initially 12.0 percent, in line with the literature (see Table 2) and by 2025 climbs to a rate of 16.2 percent. Elasticity begins at 1.49 in 1991 and fall just to

1.48 in 2025. Nevertheless, the percentage of GDP going toward health services is rising considerably slower than in Japan, but the initial ratio of health expenditures to GDP is 12.0 versus 6.8 in Japan. By 2025, the United States in this simulation has almost an equal proportion of GDP spent on health services as Japan in simulation 2 (17.1 versus 16.2), but much more than in the simulations for Japan. Thus, the growth of health expenditures is proportional to the growth of GDP.

Table S3A below lists the labor, output, market value of output in the health sector and GDP along with their respective growth rates and the elasticity of health services to GDP for the first and last four years of the time period studied.

The continuous transfer of resources from one sector of the economy to the other does not drain the productive part of the economy at a constant level and it does so at a far slower rate than in the above simulations. Later, we will compare the transfer of resources in this scenario with that of other simulations for the United States.

Table S3A

The United States: $\gamma_1 = 2\%$, $\gamma_2 = 1\%$

Year	l_2	$\dfrac{\dot{l_2}}{l_2}$ (%)	q_2	$\dfrac{\dot{q_2}}{q_2}$ (%)	y_2	$\dfrac{\dot{y_2}}{y_2}$ (%)	y	$\dfrac{\dot{y}}{y}$ (%)	Income Elasticity (%)
1990	10.49		13.50		108.00		880.00		
1991	10.57	0.76	13.77	2.00	111.02	2.80	905.04	2.85	0.98
1992	10.64	0.66	14.01	1.74	114.06	2.74	929.68	2.72	1.01
1993	10.72	0.75	14.25	1.71	117.19	2.74	954.94	2.72	1.01
2022	13.06	0.69	23.16	1.67	253.43	2.65	2006.45	2.44	1.08
2023	13.14	0.61	23.54	1.64	260.12	2.64	2055.21	2.43	1.09
2024	13.22	0.61	23.92	1.61	266.98	2.64	2104.87	2.42	1.09
2025	13.30	0.61	24.31	1.63	274.02	2.64	2155.42	2.40	1.10

8. 4 The United States Case Simulation 4

In this simulation, the growth rates of the productive sector is 2 percent, while the growth rate in the non-health sector is 0 percent. The growth rate of the aged ratio is the same as that in simulation 3, 1 percent.

1) A 2 percent productivity growth rate for the non-health sector and a 0 percent productivity growth rate for health care output will double the relative price of health sector (P_2/P_2) in the 35 years studied from 8 to 16. Since the relative price growth equals the difference in the two growth rates of productivity, the price of health services rises at a rate of 2 percent: (2% -0%). Consequently, the relative price growth follows the same course as in simulation 1 for Japan.

2) Inflation in the health sector, the rate of growth of y_2 starts out at 3.69 percent and gradually falls to 3.38. Inflation for the economy starts at 1.88 percent and slows to 1.78 percent by 2025. These rates are much higher than in simulation 3, but are more reflective of the current situation in the U.S. economy that has witnessed considerably higher inflation in the health services sector than in the rest of the economy. At this point, however, we do not draw any conclusions.

   The higher inflation in the health sector is due to the disparity in the growth rates of productivity in both sectors that is translated into higher per unit health costs in the health sector that must be financed by higher prices. Recall that in simulation 1, the difference in growth rates for the two sectors in Japan was approximately 2 percent as it is here. However, Japan's inflation rate for health services was 4.76 percent to 4.19 percent, much higher than the United States rate of 2.80 percent to 2.64 percent. This is due to the relatively higher initial level of health expenditures ($y_2 = 108$) in the U.S. compared to Japan's ($y_2 = 60$). Hence, the percentage growth is higher in Japan, even though the price levels are the same.

3) The wage rate (W) is the same in both sectors, as was discussed, and it grows at the same rate as productivity in the non-health sector (2 percent in this case). As in simulation 3, the wage rate starting at 10.30, doubles in the 35 years studied 2025. In this simulation, wages are rising slightly faster than inflation, but more so in this simulation, slower than the inflation in health services. As discussed above, this is consistent with the income elasticity greater than one, health services is a luxury good.

4) The labor force as a percentage of the population declines from 87.4 percent in 1990 [76.9 percent for non-health sector and 10.5 percent for the health sector] to 82.1 percent in 2025 [64.5 percent for non-health sector and 17.6 percent for the health sector]. This decline is a result of the aging population during the 35 year period which is increasing at the constant rate of 1.01 percent per annum. This rate is the same as in simulation 1. Specifically, labor in health initially rises at a rate of 1.6 percent and slows to a growth rate of 1.4 percent. As discussed, this slow growth rate is also a function of the different growth rates of productivity in the economy. This rate of increase is more than twice as much as in simulation 3, which is not inconsistent with the fact that the difference in the productivity rates doubles in simulation 4 to 2 percent from 1 percent.

5) The ratio of health care expenditures to GDP is rising much faster in this simulation. It is initially 12.08 percent, in line with the literature (see Table 9), and by 2025 climbs to a rate of 21.4 percent. This ratio roughly doubles in the 35 years studied. The elasticity of health services to GDP starts at 1.96 in 1991 and declines to 1.90 in 2025. This is only one-half a point higher than the same variable in simulation 3. Nevertheless, with a zero productivity growth rate, health services as a portion of GDP is higher in this scenario by the year 2025 than in either simulation for Japan, 21.4 percent versus 12.8 in simulation 1 and 17.1 in simulation 2.

Historically, the United States has doubled its proportion of GDP on health expenditures every 25 years, roughly (see Table 9). We examine this variable more closely in section 4.

Table S4A below lists the labor, output, market value of output in the health sector and GDP along with their respective growth rates and the elasticity of health services to GDP for the first and last four years of the time period studied.

The continuous transfer of resources from one sector of the economy to the other does not drain the productive part of the economy at a constant level but it appears to do so more in this simulation than in the last. Even though the labor is transferred more rapidly, those employed in the non-health sector will continue to increase output in their sector.

Table S4A

The United States: $\gamma_1 = 2\%$, $\gamma_2 = 0\%$

Year	l_2	$\dfrac{\dot{i_2}}{l_2}$ (%)	q_2	$\dfrac{\dot{q_2}}{q_2}$ (%)	y_2	$\dfrac{\dot{y_2}}{y_2}$ (%)	y	$\dfrac{\dot{y}}{y}$ (%)	Income Elasticit y (%)
1990	10.49		13.50		108.00		900.00		
1991	10.66	1.62	13.75	1.85	11.98	3.69	916.90	1.88	1.96
1992	10.83	1.59	13.97	1.60	116.05	3.63	933.87	1.85	1.96
1993	11.00	1.57	14.19	1.57	120.26	3.63	951.14	1.85	1.92
2022	16.91	1.38	21.81	1.39	328.15	3.41	1604.80		
2023	17.14	1.36	22.11	1.38	339.30	3.40	1633.46	1.79	1.90
2024	17.37	1.34	22.41	1.36	350.80	3.39	1662.60	1.78	1.90
2025	17.61	1.378	22.71	1.34	362.66	3.38	1692.21	1.78	1.90

Notes

[98] (William J. Baumol, Sue Batey Blackman and Edward N. Wolff 1989, Charles R. Hutten 1990)

[99] Economic Report of the President

CHAPTER 9

ALTERNATE SET OF ASSUMPTIONS

In the next four sections we reverse the assumed growth rates of Japan and the United States. This is done simply as an experiment to see the outcomes of both countries' variables - particularly health care inflation and the ratio of health expenditures to GDP - under different growth assumptions.

Table S5 - Simulation 5 (Japan: $\gamma_1 = 2\%$, $\gamma_2 = 1\%$)

Year	Wage	Non-health					Health					Retired	
		D_1	P_1	L_1/N	Q_1/N	Y_1/N	D_2	P_2	L_2/N	Q_2/N	Y_2/N	L_t/N	q_1/q
1990	10.00	2.00	5	82.00	164.00	820.00	1.25	8.00	6.00	7.50	60.00	11.90	22
1991	10.20	2.04	5	81.82	166.92	834.58	1.26	8.08	6.05	7.63	61.68	12.13	22
1992	10.40	2.08	5	81.54	169.68	848.39	1.28	8.16	6.09	7.76	63.33	12.37	22
1993	10.61	2.12	5	81.26	172.48	862.38	1.29	8.24	6.13	7.89	65.01	12.61	22
1994	10.82	2.16	5	80.98	175.31	876.53	1.30	8.32	6.17	8.02	66.74	12.86	22
1995	11.04	2.21	5	80.69	178.17	890.86	1.31	8.41	6.21	8.15	68.51	13.11	22
1996	11.26	2.25	5	80.39	181.07	905.36	1.33	8.49	6.24	8.29	70.32	13.36	22
1997	11.49	2.30	5	80.09	184.00	920.02	1.34	8.58	6.28	8.42	72.17	13.62	22
1998	11.72	2.34	5	79.79	186.97	934.86	1.35	8.66	6.32	8.56	74.07	13.89	22
1999	11.95	2.39	5	79.48	189.97	949.86	1.37	8.75	6.36	8.70	76.01	14.16	22
2000	12.19	2.44	5	79.17	193.00	965.02	1.38	8.84	6.40	8.84	78.00	14.44	22
2001	12.43	2.49	5	78.85	196.07	980.35	1.39	8.93	6.44	8.98	80.03	14.72	22
2002	12.68	2.54	5	78.52	199.17	995.84	1.41	9.01	6.47	9.12	82.11	15.00	22
2003	12.94	2.59	5	78.19	202.30	1011.48	1.42	9.10	6.51	9.26	84.23	15.30	22
2004	13.19	2.64	5	77.86	205.46	1027.29	1.44	9.20	6.55	9.41	86.40	15.60	22
2005	13.46	2.69	5	77.51	208.65	1043.25	1.45	9.29	6.58	9.56	88.62	15.90	22
2006	13.73	2.75	5	77.17	211.87	1059.36	1.47	9.38	6.62	9.7	90.89	16.21	22
2007	14.00	2.80	5	76.82	215.12	1075.62	1.48	9.47	6.66	9.85	93.21	16.53	22
2008	14.28	2.86	5	76.46	218.40	1092.02	1.5	9.57	6.69	10.01	95.58	16.85	22
2009	14.57	2.91	5	76.10	221.71	1108.57	1.51	9.66	6.73	10.16	98.00	17.18	22
2010	14.86	2.97	5	75.73	225.05	1125.25	1.53	9.76	6.76	10.31	100.46	17.51	22

Table S5 - Simulation 5 (Japan: $\gamma_1 = 2\%$, $\gamma_2 = 1\%$) (cont'd)

Year	Wage	Non-Health					Health					Retired	
		D_1	P_1	L_1/N	Q_1/N	Y_1/N	D_2	P_2	L_2/N	Q_2/N	Y_2/N	L_r/N	q_1/q
2011	15.16	3.03	5	75.35	228.41	1142.07	1.54	9.86	6.79	10.47	102.99	17.85	22
2012	15.46	3.09	5	74.97	231.80	1159.01	1.56	9.96	6.83	10.62	105.56	18.20	22
2013	15.77	3.15	5	74.58	235.22	1176.08	1.57	10.06	6.86	10.78	108.18	18.56	22
2014	16.08	3.22	5	74.19	238.65	1193.26	1.59	10.16	6.89	10.94	110.86	18.92	22
2015	16.41	3.28	5	73.79	242.11	1210.55	1.6	10.26	6.92	11.10	113.59	19.29	22
2016	16.73	3.35	5	73.38	245.59	1227.96	1.62	10.36	6.95	11.26	116.38	19.67	22
2017	17.07	3.41	5	72.97	249.09	1245.46	1.64	10.47	6.98	11.42	119.22	20.05	22
2018	17.41	3.48	5	72.55	252.61	1263.05	1.65	10.57	7.01	11.58	122.11	20.44	22
2019	17.76	3.55	5	72.12	256.14	1280.72	1.67	10.68	7.04	11.75	125.06	20.84	22
2020	18.11	3.62	5	71.68	259.69	1298.47	1.68	10.78	7.07	11.91	128.06	21.25	22
2021	18.48	3.70	5	71.24	263.26	1316.29	1.70	10.89	7.10	12.08	131.11	21.66	22
2022	18.85	3.77	5	70.80	266.83	1334.17	1.72	11.00	7.12	12.24	134.22	22.08	22
2023	19.22	3.84	5	70.34	270.42	1352.09	1.74	11.11	7.15	12.41	137.39	22.51	22
2024	19.61	3.92	5	69.88	274.01	1370.05	1.75	11.22	7.17	12.57	140.61	22.95	22
2025	20.00	4.00	5	69.41	277.61	1388.04	1.77	11.33	7.19	12.74	143.88	23.40	22

Note: $D_1(t) = 1.02 * D_1(t-1)$
$D_2(t) = 1.01 * D_2(t-1)$

Table S6 - Simulation 6 (Japan: γ_1 =2%, γ_2 =0%)

Year	Wage	Non-Health					Health					Retired	
		D_1	P_1	L_1/N	Q_1/N	Y_1/N	D_2	P_2	L_2/N	Q_2/N	Y_2/N	L_r/N	q_1/q_2
1990	10.00	2.00	5	82.00	164.00	820.00	1.25	8.00	6.0	7.50	60.00	11.90	22
1991	10.20	2.04	5	81.77	166.80	834.01	1.25	8.16	6.1	7.63	62.25	12.13	22
1992	10.40	2.08	5	81.43	169.44	847.22	1.25	8.32	6.2	7.75	64.50	12.37	22
1993	10.61	2.12	5	81.09	172.11	860.57	1.25	8.49	6.3	7.87	66.82	12.61	22
1994	10.82	2.16	5	80.75	174.81	874.05	1.25	8.66	6.4	7.99	69.23	12.86	22
1995	11.04	2.21	5	80.40	177.53	887.66	1.25	8.83	6.5	8.12	71.71	13.11	22
1996	11.26	2.25	5	80.04	180.28	901.4	1.25	9.01	6.6	8.24	74.28	13.36	22
1997	11.49	2.30	5	79.68	183.05	915.27	1.25	9.19	6.7	8.37	76.93	13.62	22
1998	11.72	2.34	5	79.31	185.85	929.26	1.25	9.37	6.8	8.50	79.67	13.89	22
1999	11.95	2.39	5	78.94	188.67	943.37	1.25	9.56	6.9	8.63	82.49	14.16	22
2000	12.19	2.44	5	78.56	191.52	957.6	1.25	9.75	7.01	8.76	85.41	14.44	22
2001	12.43	2.49	5	78.17	194.39	971.95	1.25	9.95	7.11	8.89	88.43	14.72	22
2002	12.68	2.54	5	77.78	197.28	986.41	1.25	10.15	7.22	9.02	91.54	15.00	22
2003	12.94	2.59	5	77.38	200.19	1000.97	1.25	10.35	7.32	9.16	94.75	15.30	22
2004	13.19	2.64	5	76.97	203.13	1015.64	1.25	10.56	7.43	9.29	98.06	15.60	22
2005	13.46	2.69	5	76.56	206.08	1030.4	1.25	10.77	7.54	9.42	101.47	15.90	22
2006	13.73	2.75	5	76.14	209.05	1045.26	1.25	10.98	7.65	9.56	104.99	16.21	22
2007	14.00	2.80	5	75.72	212.04	1060.2	1.25	11.20	7.76	9.70	108.62	16.53	22
2008	14.28	2.86	5	75.28	215.05	1075.23	1.25	11.43	7.87	9.83	112.37	16.85	22
2009	14.57	2.91	5	74.84	218.07	1090.34	1.25	11.65	7.98	9.97	116.23	17.18	22
2010	14.86	2.97	5	74.40	221.10	1105.51	1.25	11.89	8.09	10.11	120.20	17.51	22

Table S6 - Simulation 6 (Japan: γ_1 =2%, γ_2 =0%) (cont'd)

Year	Wage	Non-Health					Health					Retired	
		D_1	P_1	L_1/N	Q_1/N	Y_1/N	D_2	P_2	L_2/N	Q_2/N	Y_2/N	L_r/N	q_1/q_2
2011	15.16	3.30	5	73.94	224.15	1120.76	1.25	12.13	8.20	10.25	124.29	17.85	22
2012	15.46	3.09	5	73.48	227.21	1136.06	1.25	12.37	8.31	10.39	128.51	18.20	22
2013	15.77	3.15	5	73.02	230.28	1151.41	1.25	12.62	8.42	10.53	132.85	18.56	22
2014	16.08	3.22	5	72.54	233.36	1166.80	1.25	12.87	8.54	10.67	137.32	18.92	22
2015	16.41	3.28	5	72.06	236.45	1182.23	1.25	13.12	8.65	10.81	141.92	19.29	22
2016	16.73	3.35	5	71.57	239.54	1197.68	1.25	13.39	8.76	10.95	146.65	19.67	22
2017	17.07	3.41	5	71.07	242.63	1213.16	1.25	13.66	8.88	11.10	151.52	20.05	22
2018	17.41	3.48	5	70.57	245.73	1228.64	1.25	13.93	8.99	11.24	156.52	20.44	22
2019	17.76	3.55	5	70.06	248.82	1244.12	1.25	14.21	9.10	11.38	161.66	20.84	22
2020	18.11	3.62	5	69.54	251.92	1259.59	1.25	14.49	9.22	11.52	166.94	21.25	22
2021	18.48	3.70	5	69|01	255.01	1275.03	1.25	14.78	9.33	11.66	172.37	21.66	22
2022	18.85	3.77	5	68.48	258.09	1290.45	1.25	15.08	9.44	11.80	177.94	22.08	22
2023	19.22	3.84	5	67.93	261.16	1305.81	1.25	15.38	9.55	11.94	183.66	22.51	22
2024	19.61	3.92	5	67.38	264.22	1321.12	1.25	15.69	9.67	12.08	189.53	22.95	22
2025	20.00	4.00	5	66.82	267.27	1336.36	1.25	16.00	9.78	12.22	195.55	23.40	22

Note: $D_1(t) = 1.02*D_1(t-1)$
$D_2(t) = 1.00*D_2(t-1)$

Table S7 - Simulation 7 (The United States: $\gamma_1 = 3\%$, $\gamma_2 = 1\%$)

Year	Wage	Non-Health					Health					Retired	
		D_1	P_1	L_1/N	Q_1/N	Y_1/N	D_2	P_2	L_2/N	Q_2/N	Y_2/N	L_r/N	q_1/q_2
1990	10.30	2.06	5	76.91	158.4	792.00	1.287	8.00	10.49	13.50	108.00	12.60	12
1991	10.61	2.12	5	76.62	162.5	812.63	1.300	8.16	10.66	13.85	113.03	12.73	12
1992	10.92	2.18	5	76.32	166.8	833.76	1.313	8.32	10.83	14.22	118.29	12.85	12
1993	11.25	2.25	5	76.02	171.1	855.38	1.326	8.49	11.00	14.59	123.78	12.98	12
1994	11.59	2.32	5	75.71	175.5	877.50	1.339	8.66	11.18	14.97	129.52	13.11	12
1995	11.94	2.39	5	75.40	180.0	900.15	1.353	8.83	11.35	15.36	135.52	13.24	12
1996	12.30	2.46	5	75.09	184.7	923.32	1.366	9.01	11.53	15.76	141.79	13.38	12
1997	12.66	2.53	5	74.78	189.4	947.03	1.380	9.19	11.71	16.16	148.34	13.51	12
1998	13.04	2.61	5	74.46	194.3	971.29	1.394	9.37	11.90	16.58	155.18	13.64	12
1999	13.44	2.69	5	74.14	199.2	996.10	1.408	9.56	12.08	17.01	162.33	13.78	12
2000	13.84	2.77	5	73.81	204.3	1021.48	1.422	9.75	12.27	17.45	169.80	13.92	12
2001	14.25	2.85	5	73.48	209.5	1047.44	1.436	9.95	12.46	17.89	177.59	14.06	12
2002	14.68	2.94	5	73.15	214.8	1073.99	1.450	10.15	12.65	18.35	185.74	14.20	12
2003	15.12	3.02	5	72.82	220.2	1101.13	1.465	10.35	12.84	18.82	194.24	14.34	12
2004	15.58	3.12	5	72.48	225.8	1128.88	1.480	10.56	13.04	19.29	203.12	14.48	12
2005	16.04	3.21	5	72.13	231.4	1157.25	1.494	10.77	13.24	19.78	212.39	14.63	12
2006	16.52	3.30	5	71.79	237.2	1186.24	1.509	10.98	13.44	20.28	222.06	14.77	12
2007	17.02	3.40	5	71.44	243.2	1215.88	1.524	11.20	13.64	20.79	232.16	14.92	12
2008	17.53	3.51	5	71.08	249.2	1246.16	1.540	11.43	13.84	21.32	242.70	15.07	12
2009	18.06	3.61	5	70.73	255.4	1277.10	1.555	11.65	14.05	21.85	253.70	15.22	12
2010	18.60	3.72	5	70.37	261.7	1308.72	1.571	11.89	14.26	22.39	265.18	15.37	12

Table S7 - Simulation 7 (The United States: $\gamma_1 =3\%$, $\gamma_2 =1\%$) (cont'd)

| Year | Wage | Non-Health | | | | | | Health | | | | | | | Retired | | |
		D_1	P_1	L_1/N	Q_1/N	Y_1/N	D_2	P_2	L_2/N	Q_2/N	Y_2/N			L_r/N	q_1/q_2
2011	19.16	3.83	5	70.00	268.2	1341.01	1.586	12.13	14.47	22.95	277.16			15.53	12
2012	19.73	3.95	5	69.64	274.8	1373.99	1.602	12.37	14.68	23.52	289.66			15.68	12
2013	20.32	4.06	5	69.27	281.5	1407.68	1.618	12.62	14.89	24.10	302.70			15.84	12
2014	20.93	4.19	5	68.89	288.4	1442.08	1.634	12.87	15.11	24.70	316.29			16.00	12
2015	21.56	4.31	5	68.51	295.4	1477.20	1.651	13.12	15.33	25.30	330.48			16.16	12
2016	22.21	4.44	5	68.13	302.6	1513.05	1.667	13.39	15.55	25.92	345.27			16.32	12
2017	22.87	4.57	5	67.75	309.9	1549.64	1.684	13.66	15.77	26.55	360.69			16.48	12
2018	23.56	4.71	5	67.36	317.4	1586.99	1.701	13.93	15.99	27.20	376.77			16.65	12
2019	24.27	4.85	5	66.97	325.0	1625.10	1.718	14.21	16.22	27.86	393.53			16.81	12
2020	24.99	5.00	5	66.57	332.8	1663.98	1.735	14.49	16.44	28.53	411.01			16.98	12
2021	25.74	5.15	5	66.17	340.7	1703.64	1.752	14.78	16.67	29.21	429.22			17.15	12
2022	26.52	5.30	5	65.77	348.8	1744.10	1.770	15.08	16.90	29.91	448.20			17.32	12
2023	27.31	5.46	5	65.37	357.1	1785.36	1.788	15.38	17.13	30.63	467.98			17.50	12
2024	28.13	5.63	5	64.96	365.5	1827.43	1.805	15.69	17.37	31.36	488.59			17.67	12
2025	28.98	5.80	5	64.55	374.1	1870.32	1.823	16.00	17.60	32.10	510.06			17.85	12

Note: $D_1(t) = 1.03*D_1(t-1)$
$D_2(t) = 1.01*D_2(t-1)$

Table S8 - Simulation 8 (The United States: $\gamma_1 = 3\%$, $\gamma_2 = 0\%$)

Year	Wage	Non-Health					Health					Retired	
		D_1	P_1	L_1/N	Q_1/N	Y_1/N	D_2	P_2	L_2/N	Q_2/N	Y_2/N	L_r/N	q_1/q_2
1990	10.3	2.06	5	76.91	158.4	792.00	1.287	8.00	10.49	13.50	108.00	12.60	12
1991	10.61	2.12	5	76.53	162.3	811.66	1.287	8.24	10.75	13.84	114.00	12.73	12
1992	10.92	2.18	5	76.13	166.3	831.72	1.287	8.49	11.01	14.18	120.32	12.85	12
1993	11.25	2.25	5	75.73	170.4	852.18	1.287	8.74	11.28	14.53	126.98	12.98	12
1994	11.59	2.32	5	75.33	174.6	873.04	1.287	9.00	11.56	14.88	133.99	13.11	12
1995	11.94	2.39	5	74.91	178.9	894.30	1.287	9.27	11.84	15.24	141.37	13.24	12
1996	12.30	2.46	5	74.50	183.2	915.97	1.287	9.55	12.13	15.61	149.14	13.38	12
1997	12.66	2.53	5	74.07	187.6	938.05	1.287	9.84	12.42	15.99	157.32	13.51	12
1998	13.04	2.61	5	73.64	192.1	960.55	1.287	10.13	12.72	16.37	165.93	13.64	12
1999	13.44	2.69	5	73.20	196.7	983.46	1.287	10.44	13.02	16.76	174.98	13.78	12
2000	13.84	2.77	5	72.75	201.4	1006.78	1.287	10.75	13.33	17.16	184.50	13.92	12
2001	14.25	2.85	5	72.30	206.1	1030.52	1.287	11.07	13.65	17.57	194.52	14.06	12
2002	14.68	2.94	5	71.84	210.9	1054.67	1.287	11.41	13.97	17.98	205.05	14.20	12
2003	15.12	3.02	5	71.37	215.8	1079.24	1.287	11.75	14.29	18.40	216.12	14.34	12
2004	15.58	3.12	5	70.89	220.8	1104.23	1.287	12.10	14.62	18.82	227.76	14.48	12
2005	16.04	3.21	5	70.41	225.9	1129.64	1.287	12.46	14.96	19.26	239.99	14.63	12
2006	16.52	3.30	5	69.92	231.1	1155.46	1.287	12.84	15.30	19.70	252.84	14.77	12
2007	17.02	3.40	5	69.43	236.3	1181.70	1.287	13.22	15.65	20.14	266.34	14.92	12
2008	17.53	3.51	5	68.93	241.7	1208.35	1.287	13.62	16.00	20.60	280.52	15.07	12
2009	18.06	3.61	5	68.42	247.1	1235.40	1.287	14.03	16.36	21.06	295.40	15.22	12
2010	18.60	3.72	5	67.90	252.6	1262.87	1.287	14.45	16.72	21.53	311.03	15.37	12

Table S8 - Simulation 8 (The United States: γ_1 =3%, γ_2 =0%) (cont'd)

Year	Wage	Non-Health					Health					Retired	
		D_1	P_1	L_1/N	Q_1/N	Y_1/N	D_2	P_2	L_2/N	Q_2/N	Y_2/N	L_r/N	q_1/q_2
2011	19.16	3.83	5	67.38	258.1	1290.74	1.287	14.88	17.09	22.00	327.43	15.53	12
2012	19.73	3.95	5	66.85	263.8	1319.01	1.287	15.33	17.47	22.48	344.64	15.68	12
2013	20.32	4.06	5	66.31	269.5	1347.68	1.287	15.79	17.85	22.97	362.70	15.84	12
2014	20.93	4.19	5	65.77	275.3	1376.74	1.287	16.26	18.23	23.47	381.63	16.00	12
2015	21.56	4.31	5	65.22	281.2	1406.19	1.287	16.75	18.62	23.97	401.49	16.16	12
2016	22.21	4.44	5	64.66	287.2	1436.01	1.287	17.25	19.02	24.48	422.30	16.32	12
2017	22.87	4.57	5	64.10	293.2	1466.21	1.287	17.77	19.42	24.99	444.12	16.48	12
2018	23.56	4.71	5	63.53	299.4	1496.78	1.287	18.30	19.82	25.51	466.98	16.65	12
2019	24.27	4.85	5	62.95	305.5	1527.70	1.287	18.85	20.23	26.04	490.93	16.81	12
2020	24.99	5.00	5	62.87	311.8	1558.98	1.287	19.42	20.64	26.57	516.01	16.98	12
2021	25.74	5.15	5	61.78	318.1	1590.60	1.287	20.00	21.06	27.11	542.27	17.15	12
2022	26.52	5.30	5	61.19	324.5	1622.55	1.287	20.60	21.49	27.66	569.75	17.32	12
2023	27.31	5.46	5	60.59	331.0	1654.82	1.287	21.22	21.91	28.21	598.52	17.50	12
2024	28.13	5.63	5	59.98	337.5	1687.40	1.287	21.86	22.35	28.76	628.61	17.67	12
2025	28.98	5.80	5	59.37	344.1	1720.29	1.287	22.51	22.78	29.32	660.09	17.85	12

Note: $D_1(t) = 1.03*D_1(t-1)$
$D_2(t) = 1.00*D_2(t-1)$

9.1 Japan: Simulation 5

In this simulation, the growth rate of the productive sector is 2 percent, while the growth rate in the non-health sector is 1 percent. The growth rate of the aged ratio is the same as that in simulation 1 and 2, 1.95 percent.

The growth rate of GDP is considerably slower than in simulation 1 and 2. This is due to both the lower growth rate of productivity in the non-health sector and the constant ratio of output, q_1/q_2 that controls among other things, the transfer of labor. Comparing simulations 5 and 6 with 1 and 2, one can see an equal growth rate of GDP between the two sets of simulations (1 and 2, and 5 and 6), but a different growth rate across the two sets. This difference is related to both the growth rate of productivity in the non-health sector and the constant ratio of output q_1/q_2. This feature is also found in the 4 simulations for the United States.

1) A 2 percent productivity growth rate for the non-health sector and 1 percent productivity growth rate for health care output allows for a slower growth in the relative price of the health sector (P_2/P_2) in the 35 years studied from 8 to 11.33. Since the relative price growth equals the difference in the two growth rates of productivity, the price of health services rises at a rate of 1 percent: (2% - 1%). Recall in simulation 1, the relative price doubled in the 35 year period. Consequently, the relative price growth is much less severe than in previous simulations for Japan.

2) Inflation in the health sector, the rate of growth of y_2 starts out at 2.8 percent and gradually falls to 2.33 percent. This is also significantly lower than the inflation in this sector in the first simulation. In fact, its slightly more than one-half the inflation rate for the health sector in simulation 1. Inflation for the economy starts at 1.85 percent and slows to 1.41 percent by 2025. These rates are also less than in those in sumulation 1 (2.85% to 2.4%).

Thus, we show that if we change the assumption about the growth rate in productivity, the impact on the inflation rate of the health sector changes considerably. This is based on the relationship of the growth of the labor costs across both sectors due to productivity in the non-health sector and how the health sector absorbs these costs through raising its price.

Note also that the growth rate of output in health services q_2 is a whole percentage point less than that of simulation 1, even though both share the same productivity growth rate: $\gamma_2 = 1\%$.

Table S5A – Japan: $\gamma_1 = 2\%$, $\gamma_2 = 1\%$

Year	l_2	i_2/l_2	q_2	$\dot{q}_2/q_2$	y_2	$\dot{y}_2/y_2$	y	$\dot{y}/y$	y_2/y (%)	$\dfrac{(y_2\dot{}/y)}{(y_2/y)}$	Income Elasticity
1990	6.00		7.50		60.00		880.00		6.818182		
1991	6.05	0.83%	7.63	1.73%	61.68	2.80%	896.26	1.85%	6.881672	0.93%	1.51%
1992	6.09	0.66%	7.76	1.70%	63.33	2.68%	911.72	1.73%	6.945708	0.93%	1.55%
1993	6.13	0.66%	7.89	1.68%	65.01	2.65%	927.39	1.72%	7.010296	0.93%	1.55%
2022	7.12	0.28%	12.24	1.32%	134.22	2.37%	1468.39		9.140916		
2023	7.15	0.42%	12.41	1.39%	137.39	2.36%	1489.48	1.44%	9.223894	0.91%	1.64%
2024	7.17	0.28%	12.57	1.29%	140.61	2.34%	1510.66	1.42%	9.307547	0.91%	1.65%
2025	7.19	0.28%	12.74	1.35%	143.88	2.33%	1531.92	1.41%	9.391881	0.91%	1.65%

Table S6A – Japan: $\gamma_1 = 2\%$, $\gamma_2 = 0\%$

Year	l_2	i_2/l_2	q_2	$\dot{q}_2/q_2$	y_2	$\dot{y}_2/y_2$	y	$\dot{y}/y$	y_2/y (%)	$\dfrac{(y_2\dot{}/y)}{(y_2/y)}$	Income Elasticity
1990	6.00		7.50		60.00		880.00		6.82		
1991	6.10	1.67%	7.63	1.73%	62.25	3.75%	896.26	1.85%	6.95	1.87%	2.03%
1992	6.20	1.64%	7.75	1.57%	64.50	3.61%	911.72	1.72%	7.07	1.86%	2.10%
1993	6.30	1.61%	7.87	1.55%	66.82	3.60%	927.39	1.72%	7.21	1.85%	2.09%
2022	9.44	1.18%	11.80	1.20%	177.94	3.23%	1468.39	1.45%	12.12	1.75%	2.23%
2023	9.55	1.17%	11.94	1.19%	183.66	3.21%	1489.48	1.44%	12.33	1.75%	2.24%
2024	9.67	1.26%	12.08	1.17%	189.53	3.20%	1510.66	1.42%	12.55	1.75%	2.25%
2025	9.78	1.14%	12.22	1.16%	195.55	3.18%	1531.92	1.41%	12.77	1.74%	2.26%

3) The wage rate (W) is the same in both sectors, as was discussed, and it grows at the same rate as productivity in the non-health sector (2 percent in this case). As in simulation 1, the wage rate starting at 10.00, doubles in the 35 years studied. In this simulation, wages are also rising faster than inflation, and slower than the inflation in health services, a finding that was consistent in all the above simulations.

4) The labor force as a percentage of the population declines from 88.0 percent in 1990 [82.0 percent for non-health sector and 6.0 percent for the health sector] to 76.6 percent in 2025 [69.4 percent for non-health sector and 7.2 percent for the health sector]. This decline is a result of the aging population during the 35 year period which is increasing at the constant rate of 1.95 percent per annum. There is nothing different about this statistic from simulations 1 and 2 as the assumption concerning the growth rate of the elderly does not change.

What does change is the labor breakdown. Recall the transfer rate of labor is a function of $\gamma_1-\gamma_2$ which in this simulation is 1%. Thus the growth rate of the labor force in health initially rises at a rate of 0.83 percent and slows to a growth rate of 0.28 percent. This is less than one-half the growth rate found in simulation 1. Thus, the slower price rise is consistent with a lower growth rate in the labor force. Note, however, that since there is a productivity growth rate in health care in this simulation, the per unit of output labor costs are dampened somewhat than in the following simulation.

5) The ratio of health care expenditures to GDP is rising slightly slower in this simulation for Japan. It is initially 6.82 percent, in line with the literature and by 2025 climbs to a rate of 9.4 percent. This elasticity of health expenditures starts at 1.52 in 1991 and rises to 1.65 in 2025. This is not significantly different from the elasticity measurement in simulation 1 (1.68 and 1.74). A lower disparity in the growth rates of productivity, however, generates an elasticity rate that rises faster in health services as a portion of GDP.

Table S5A lists the labor, output, market value of output in the health sector and GDP along with their respective growth rates and the elasticity of health services to GDP for the first and last four years of the time period studied.

Here the transfer of resources from one sector of the economy to the other maintains a slower decline in the productive part of the economy.

9.2   Japan: Simulation 6

In this simulation, the growth rate of the productive sector is 2 percent, while the growth rate in the non-health sector is 0 percent. The growth rate of the aged ratio is the same as that in simulation 5, 1.95 percent.

The growth rate of GDP is the same as that in simulation 5, as discussed above.

1)   A 2 percent productivity growth rate for the non-health sector and a 0 percent productivity growth rate for health care output will double the relative price of health sector (P_2/P_1) in the 35 years studied from 8 to 16. Since the relative price growth equals the difference in the two growth rates of productivity, the price of health services rises at a rate of 2 percent: (2% - 0%). Consequently, the relative price growth follows the same course as in simulation 1 for Japan where $\gamma_1-\gamma_2$ also equaled 2 percent.

2)   Inflation in the health sector, the rate of growth of y_2 starts out at 3.75 percent and gradually falls to 3.18 percent. Inflation for the economy starts at 1.87 percent and slows to 1.74 percent by 2025. These rates are much higher than in simulation 5, but still less than that of simulation 1.

3)   The wage rate (W) is the same in both sectors, as was discussed, and it grows at the same rate as productivity in the non-health sector (2 percent in this case). As in simulation 5, the wage rate starting at 10.00, doubles in the 35 years studied until 2025. In this simulation, wages are rising slightly faster than inflation, but now they rise significantly slower than the inflation in health services in simulation 5.

Coincidentally, the doubling of the wage rate in the 35 year period is similar to that of the United States in simulations 3 and 4 where γ_1 = 2 percent but γ_2 = 1 percent.

4)   The labor force as a percentage of the population declines from 88.0 percent in 1990 [82 percent for non-health sector and 6 percent for the health sector] to 76.6 percent in 2025 [66.8 percent for non-health sector and 9.78 percent for the health sector]. Specifically, labor in health initially rises at a rate of 1.67 percent and slows to a growth rate of 1.14 percent. The greater difference in growth rates of productivity in the economy forces more labor into the health sector over time. This rate of increase is almost a whole percentage point higher than in simulation 5, which is not inconsistent with the fact that the difference in

the productivity rates doubles in simulation 6 to 2 percent from 1 percent. This is consistent with the United States in simulations 3 and 4. In addition, the growth rate of l_2 mimics that found in simulation 1.

5) The ratio of health care expenditures to GDP is rising much faster in this simulation, but the elasticity of health services to GDP follows a similar pattern as that in simulation 2. It is initially 6.82 percent, and by 2025 climbs to a rate of 12.8 percent. This ratio roughly doubles in the 35 years studied. This is exactly the course followed in simulation 1 when in fact the difference in productivity growth rates $(\gamma_1-\gamma_2)$ was also 2 percent. The elasticity is 2.03 in 1991 and rises to 2.26. Again, this is only one-half a point more in simulation 5. Moreover, the pattern of simulations 6 and 5 are remarkably similar to simulations 1 and 2, but interestingly not quite as smooth.

Table S6A lists the labor, output, market value of output in the health sector and GDP along with their respective growth rates and the elasticity of health services to GDP for the first and last four years of the time period studied.

Japan's 1st period inflation rate for health services jumps from 4.8 percent in simulation 1 to 5.7 percent in simulation 2. In simulations 5 and 6, it moves from 2.8 percent to 3.7 percent. This is a full two percentage points lower when the productivity in the noon-health sector drops from 3 percent to 2 percent. Inflation in the GDP moves from 2.85 in simulations 1 and 2 (recall the growth rates are the same) to 1.85 percent, or a one percentage point difference. Thus the higher disparity in the growth rates of productivity between the non-health and health sectors has a large impact on the cost movement of health services. This is precisely due to the pressure from wage growth that accompanies the high productivity in the non-health sector. Moreover, even though health expenditures remains less than 10 percent of the GDP, this disparity will have an impact on inflation in the economy. When comparing wage increases relative to health expenditures, a higher productivity disparity makes it more difficult to afford the rising costs of health services, as both the US and Japan's economy has seen. Nevertheless, this phenomenon of soaring health costs can be supported by the economy as output in both sectors is rising and wages rise faster than overall inflation.

9.3 The United States: Simulation 7

In this simulation, the growth rate of the productive sector is 3 percent, while the growth rate in the non-health sector is 1 percent. The growth rate of the aged ratio is the same as that in simulation 3 and 4, 1 percent.

1) A 3 percent productivity growth rate for the non-health sector and a 1 percent productivity growth rate for health care output doubles the price of the health sector (P_2/P_1) in the 35 years studied from 8 to 16. We saw this pattern in simulations 1, 4 and 6 when the difference in productivity growth ($\gamma_1-\gamma_2$) also measure 2 percent: 3% -1%. Recall that the initial relative price set for Japan and the United States was $P_1 = 5$ and $P_2 = 8$ for both countries.

2) Inflation in the health sector, the rate of growth of y_2 starts out at 4.7 percent and gradually falls to 4.4 percent. This is significantly more than the inflation in this sector for simulation 3. In fact, these rates are almost 2 percentage points higher than simulations 3 and 4 when the difference in productivity growth rates was also 2 percent. Inflation for the whole economy goes from 2.9 percent to 2.8 percent. This is also the case in simulation 8. This inflation rate is a full percentage point higher than the rate found in simulation 4.

   Thus we show that if we change the assumption about the growth rate in productivity, the impact on the inflation rate of the health sector changes considerably. This is based on the relationship of the productivity of the non-health sector on the growth of the labor costs across both sectors. The health sector absorbs these costs through raising its price, and this higher price of health along with the growing demand for health services places a higher and higher drain on the economy. This is seen in the growing health expenditures to GDP. Nevertheless, the economy is able to support this rising health burden.

   Note, the growth rate of output in health services q_2 is higher than that of simulation 3, even though they both share the same productivity growth rate: $\gamma_2 = 1\%$. This difference is less than a percentage point, slight less of change that that found in Japan's simulations for $\gamma_2 = 1\%$. Like simulations 2, 4 and 6, q_2 rises at the same rate as l_2 since $\gamma_2 = 0$.

3) The wage rate (W) is the same in both sectors, as was discussed, and it grows at the same rate as productivity in the non-health sector (3 percent in this case). The wage rate starting at 10.30, doubles in the 24 years and reaches 28.98 in 2025. In this simulation, wages rise just faster than inflation (3.0% versus 2.9%), and slower than the inflation in health services. In both, this simulation and the one that follows, the difference in these two very important growth measurements - wage growth over inflation, are closer than in any other set of simulations.

4) The labor force as a percentage of the population declines from 87.4 percent in 1990 [76.9 percent for non-health sector and 10.5 percent for the health sector] to 82.2 percent in 2025 [64.6 percent for non-health sector and 17.6 percent for the health sector]. This decline is a result of the aging population during the 35 year period which is increasing at the constant rate of 1 percent per annum. Both the relative size of the labor force and the breakdown is the same as that in simulation 4 since assumption concerning the growth rate of the elderly is still 1 percent and the difference in productivity growth rates $(\gamma_1 - \gamma_2)$, which determines the transfer of labor as described in the appendix, is also the same (2 percent).

5) The ratio of health care expenditures to GDP is rising much faster in these simulations. It is initially 12 percent, and by 2025 climbs to a rate of 21.4 percent. This ratio is growing at a rate starting at 1.7 percent in 1991 and declining to 1.6 percent in 2025. This is roughly the elasticity measure is smooth in these simulations, but not quite as smooth as those in simulations 3 and 4. It starts at 1.64 percent and slows to a rate of 1.58 percent. Again, however, the elasticity measure for the United States is declining slightly, when the same statistic in the simulations for Japan are increasing.

Table S7A below lists the labor, output, market value of output in the health sector and GDP along with their respective growth rates and the elasticity of health services to GDP for the first and last four years of the time period studied.

Here the transfer of resources from one sector of the economy to the other contributes to a faster decline in the productive part of the economy.

Table S7A – The United States: $\gamma_1 = 3\%$, $\gamma_2 = 1\%$

Year	l_2	$\dot{l}_2/l_2$ (%)	q_2	$\dot{q}_2/q_2$ (%)	y_2	$\dot{y}_2/y_2$ (%)	y	$\dot{y}/y$ (%)	Income Elasticity
1990	10.49		13.50		108.00		900.00		
1991	10.66	1.62	13.85	2.59	113.03	4.66	925.66	2.90	1.64%
1992	10.83	1.59	14.22	2.67	118.29	4.65	952.05	2.80	1.64%
1993	11.00	1.57	14.59	2.60	123.78	4.64	979.16	2.80	1.64%
2022	16.90	1.38	29.91	2.40	448.20	4.42	2192.30		
2023	17.13	1.36	30.63	2.41	467.98	4.41	2253.34	2.80	1.81%
2024	17.37	1.40	31.36	2.38	488.59	4.40	2316.02	2.80	1.81%
2025	17.60	1.32	32.10	2.36	510.06	4.39	2380.38	2.80	1.81%

9.4 The United States: Simulation 8

In this simulation, the growth rate of the productive sector is 3 percent, while the growth rate in the non-health sector is 0 percent. The growth rate of the aged ratio is the same as that in simulation 7, 1 percent.

1) A 3 percent productivity growth rate for the non-health sector and a 0 percent productivity growth rate for health care output doubles the price of the health sector (P_2/P_1) in 24 years, and the price ratio reaches 22.51 in 2025. We saw this exact pattern in simulations 2 when the difference in productivity growth ($\gamma_1-\gamma_2$)also measured 3 percent.

2) Inflation in the health sector, the rate of growth of y_2, starts out at 5. 6 percent and gradually falls to 5.0 percent. This is significantly more than that found in both simulation 7 and 2. What is interesting is to compare it to simulation 2 for Japan. When Japan's model had growth rates of productivity of 3% and 0%, its growth rate of health expenditures started at 5.72 percent but declined faster to a growth rate of 4.95 percent. Hence, the growth patterns in the United States are much smoother. Moreover, when comparing the United States' growth rates in simulation 7 and 8 with Japan's in 1 and 2, the increase for the Untied States from simulation 7 to 8 is slightly smaller than that for Japan (an average per-centage point difference of 0.2). Inflation for the whole economy goes from 2.9 percent to 2.8 percent. This is also the case in simulation 7. This inflation rate pattern, although it starts out the same, is also much smoother than Japan's in simulations 1 and 2.

Note, the growth rate of output in health services q_2 is very similar to that of simulation 7. This pattern is similar to simulations 3 and 4 as well as 1 and 2; however, it is much smoother.

3) The wage rate (W) is the same in both sectors, and it grows at the same rate as productivity in the non-health sector or 3 percent. The wage rate starting at 10.30, doubles in the 24 years and reaches 28.98 in 2025. In this simulation similar to simulation 7, wages rise just faster than inflation (3.0% versus 2.9%), yet significantly slower than the inflation in health services. As mentioned above, the difference in these two growth measurements-wage growth over in-flation are closer than in any other set of simulations.

4) The labor force as a percentage of the population declines from 87.4 percent in 1990 [76.9 percent for non-health sector and 10.5 percent for the health sector]

to 82.2 percent in 2025 [59.4 percent for non-health sector and 22.8 percent for the health sector]. Although the total labor force is the same in this simulation as that in simulation 7 as well as 3 and 4 due to the constant rate of aging to 1 percent per annum, the rate of transfer for labor is changed. The rate of growth of labor in health services is almost a full percentage point higher than that in simulation 7.

5) The ratio of health care expenditures to GDP is rising faster in this simulation. It is initially 12 percent, and by 2025 climbs to a rate of 27.7 percent- more than one-quarter of the United States' economy! The elasticity starts at 1.95 percent and declines slightly to 1.8 percent in 2025. Again, the elasticity measure is smoother in these simulations. Once again, however, the elasticity measure for the United States is declining slightly, but the same statistic in the simulations for Japan are increasing.

Table S8A below lists the labor, output, market value of output in the health sector and GDP along with their respective growth rates and the elasticity of health services to GDP for the first and last four years of the time period studied.

Table S8A – The United States: $y_1 = 3\%$, $\gamma_2 = 0\%$

Year	l_2	$\dot{l}_2/l_2$ (%)	q_2	$\dot{q}_2/q_2$ (%)	y_2	$\dot{y}_2/y_2$ (%)	y	$\dot{y}/y$ (%)	Income Elasticity
1990	10.49		13.50		108.00		900.00		
1991	10.75	2.48	13.84	2.52	114.00	5.56	925.66	2.85	1.95%
1992	11.01	2.42	14.18	2.46	120.32	5.54	952.05	2.85	1.95%
1993	11.28	2.45	14.53	2.47	126.98	5.54	979.16	2.85	1.94%
2022	21.49	2.04	27.66	2.03	569.75	5.07	2192.30	2.79	
2023	21.91	1.95	28.21	1.99	598.52	5.05	2253.34	2.78	1.81%
2024	22.35	2.01	28.76	1.95	628.61	5.03	2316.02	2.78	1.81%
2025	22.78	1.95	29.32	1.95	660.09	5.01	2380.38	2.78	1.81%

CHAPTER 10

CONCLUDING REMARKS AND POLICY RECOMMENDATIONS

In our model, we addressed the acceleration of health care costs through simulations of the effect of the wage pressure-component of health care inflation and the growing aging population on the health care industry as well as other more productive industries. Our simulations support the assertion that higher productivity growth rates in the non-health sectors will help to absorb the anticipated higher health care costs of the future. Our model shows that under realistic productivity assumptions for both the U.S. and Japan the two economies are able to support the continually escalating health care costs as long as we maintain adequate productivity levels in other sectors of the economy.

Health care services can indeed withstand the growing demand of the aging population, even in the case where the price of health care services doubles, as long as productivity in all other sectors rises at a consistent rate that enables society to absorb these prices. The U.S. and Japan will be able to afford the increasing costs of health care brought on by the aging population, economic growth (which increases income and demand) and health care price inflation as long as productivity gains in other sectors are transferred properly to the health care sector via equal wage increases between sectors.

Our monograph offers an alternative[100] policy recommendation for health care cost concerns of the future. Policy alternatives should be evaluated in terms of their effectiveness in containing and/or absorbing costs, their acceptability by patients and health care providers, and their administrative and political feasibility (they should be relatively easy to administer and they should be able to elicit political support from major interest groups).

Our policy recommendation meets all these criteria. Increasing and/or maintaining productivity levels in the non-health care sectors of the economy is the most effective way of absorbing future health care costs. Increasing productivity in the health care sector is the most effective way of containing health care costs. Regarding the acceptability of the second part of our previous recommendation we have to make the following clarification.

Undoubtedly, a more rapid rate of productivity growth in the health care sector itself increases efficiency and thereby mitigates high health care costs in the future. Unfortunately, though, patients might be concerned about the need of an assembly-line medical treatment process to bring about such productivity gains. Mechanization of health care services jeopardize the quality of these services and makes the anticipated productivity gains unacceptable. In our recommendation, we want to clarify that not all health care services are inherently hostile to productivity growth. Productivity growth does not always have to come at the expense of quality. The technology of the supply process in different health care services is different and the productivity growth rate could be different. Adopting Baumol's (1985)[101] taxonomy of service activities we could differentiate between *stagnant personal health care services, progressive impersonal health care services, and asymptotically stagnant impersonal health care services.*

Stagnant personal health care services are those provided by doctors and nurses where there must be direct contact between patients and providers and where quality of service is highly correlated with labor-time expended by the service providers. Such services resist productivity-enhancing change because the loss of quality that would result from changing the technology of their supply process is obvious enough. Mechanization of the health care supply process in order to achieve assembly-line medical treatment and reduction in the amount of time devoted by the providers is not only undesirable but in some cases even unacceptable. We do agree that overall productivity in the supply of such personal health care services cannot increase fast enough to pay for the wage increases of the providers over time.

Progressive impersonal health care services are those services provided by pharmaceutical companies, blood test labs, etc., where no contact between patients and providers is necessary in the supply process. Technological innovation can yield high productivity growth in the production process of these impersonal health care services and pay for the wage increases of their providers.

Asymptotically stagnant impersonal services are those services provided by auxiliary equipment used by nurses and physicians in the production process of their services. The auxiliary equipment is derived from the productivity progressive sector of the economy whereas the services of nurses and doctors are derived from the productivity stagnant sector of the economy. For decades, the ability of auxiliary equipment to help with the diagnosis and treatment of medical problems has expanded drastically and, as a result, equipment cost per unit of output has declined significantly. At the same time, the cost of nurses and physicians who use this equipment has been rising. In such cases, the combined productivity can partially pay for the wage increases of nurses and physicians.

We expect that some productivity growth in health care services would be acceptable by both patients and physicians, especially when such productivity gains could be obtained without any sacrifice of quality.

Our recommendation definitely meets the criterion of administrative feasibility. It is relatively easy to monitor productivity trends[102] in different sectors of the economy and introduce measures that maximize productive efficiency. The Bureau of Labor Statistics of the U.S. Department of Labor already monitors and publishes[103] estimates of productivity measures for different sectors of the U.S. economy and the economies of other industrialized countries. Among other recommendations, the 1990 proposals of the Brookings Institution[104] and the 1994 proposals published by the American Management Association[105] recommend practical measures to secure productivity growth in different sectors of the economy. Similar practical measures to secure productivity gains have been also recommended by private professionals in a host of publications.[106]

Our recommendation also meets the criterion of political feasibility. It is expected that major interest groups such as labor, business, insurance, physicians, hospitals, and consumer groups such as senior citizens' organizations, along with state and local government officials will provide political support to our recommendation because it provides freedom of choice. Under our recommendation of sustained current trends of productivity growth, health care services will continue to be provided predominantly by private nonprofit or for-profit organizations and the patients will continue to have the option of selection from a mix of fee-for-service and prepaid modes of practice.

This monograph has addressed the key dilemmas that must be confronted if health care financing is to achieve a degree of acceptance in both, the Japanese and the U.S. health care cultures. It offers alternative scenarios of proactive measures to the health care financing dilemma that are equitable and tolerable by consumers, providers and payors.

Our model indicates that the growth rate in the relative price of the health sector (P_2/P_1) is equal to the difference in the productivity growth rates of the health sector and of all other sectors of the economy. The policy implication of this finding is illustrated in our simulation Tables. The higher the productivity growth rate in the health sector the easier it gets for all other sectors of the economy to absorb future increases in health care costs. For example, a 3 percent productivity growth rate for the non-health care sector will double the relative price of the health sector (P_2/P_1) in 35 years when the productivity growth rate for health care output is 1 percent, and in 24 years when the productivity growth rate for health care output is 0 percent. Such productivity gains for the health care sector could come from the *progressive impersonal health care services and asymptotically stagnant impersonal health care services*. Productivity estimates by Bureau of Labor Statistics of the U.S. Department of Labor[107] indicate that the annual percentage change in productivity for medical services provided by the U.S. Federal Government increased from 0.4 percent during the 1967-1990 period to 0.8 percent during the 1985-1990 period.[108] The percentage change for the 1989-1990 period was 0.4 percent. This positive increase indicates that productivity gains are feasible in the health care sector and should be expected to continue in the future. The higher the productivity gains in the supply of health care services the lower the price inflation rate of that sector. A higher productivity growth rate is translated into lower labor costs per unit of output which is then passed on to consumers via lower prices.

The magnitude of the productivity growth rate of health care services has also important implications for the size of the income elasticity of demand for health care services and, hence, the economy's allocation of resources on this sector. The higher the health care productivity gains the lower the income elasticity of demand for health care services and the lower the percentage of GDP that is allocated to health care services.

Notes

[100] For a good review of past policy recommendations see: Davis, Karen, Gerard P. Anderson, Diane Rowland, Earl P. Steinberg (1990).

[101] Baumol, William J. (1985), Chapter 11, pp. 301-318

[102] For a good introduction to productivity measurement issues, see: Japan Productivity Center, (1984)

[103] See different issues of the *Monthly Labor Review*, published by U.S. Department of Labor, Bureau of Labor Statistic.

[104] See: Blinder, Alan S. (1990).

[105] See: Sibson, Robert E. (1994)
[106] See, for example: Fazzi, Robert A. (1994)
[107] See: Dumas, Mark W. (1992)
[108] Percentage changes for a manufacturing sector such as primary aluminum was 3.1 per-
       cent during the 1947-1990 period, 3.0 percent during the 1985-1990 period and 5.7 per-
       cent during 1989-1990 period.

Appendix A
Specification of the Model

1.1 ASSUMPTIONS

Industrial Make-up of the Model

There are two sectors in the economy: non health and health. The non-health sector is progressive with respect to productivity, and the health sector is stagnant. Let D_i ($i = 1$ and 2) be the productivity of sector i where $i = 1$ for the non-health sector and $i = 2$ for the health sector. The growth rate of productivity is defined as

$$\dot{D}_i / D_i = \gamma_i \qquad i = 1, 2 \tag{1.1}$$

1. We assume the productivity growth is constant for both sectors, $i = 1$and
2. If the growth rate of productivity is positive then output per unit of input is rising every year.

$$\gamma_i = c_i \quad constant \quad i = 1, 2$$

2. Productivity in the non-health sector grows at a faster rate than that in the health sector.

$$\gamma_1 > \gamma_2 \geq 0 \tag{1.2}$$

Wages, Labor Mobility, Output

Wage rates are the same for both sectors. This is a result of freedom of labor mobility, and homogeneity of labor as described in the assumptions section (see section # 3), i.e.

$$W_1 = W_2 = W \tag{1.3}$$

Total GDP, Y, is given as

$$Y = Y_1 + Y_2 = P_1.Q_1 + P_2.Q_2 = W(L_1 + L_2) \qquad (1.4)$$

where Y_i is the market value of output, P_i is the price of output, Q_i is the quantity of output and L_i is the labor force used for sectors $i = 1$ and 2. Total GDP, Y, is the sum of the market values of the total output in both sectors. It is also equal to the national income which is paid to the factor of production, in this case labor, multiplied by the wage rate. In other words, all income in the economy is earned by the labor force in the form of wages. All that is produced is consumed in the same period. There is no saving nor borrowing, no profits, and no taxes nor transfers. Let L_r be the number of retired people in the total population, N,so that total population is the sum of retired persons and the labor force. Hence,

$$N = L_1 + L_2 + L_r \qquad (1.5)$$

Unemployment is 0. If we normalize the variables by dividing by total population N, we get per capita output, per capita GDP, as well as the relative labor and elderly ratio.

$$
\begin{aligned}
Y/N &= y & Y_i/N = y_i \qquad Q_i/N = q_i, & \qquad for \quad i = 1,2 \\
L_i/N &= l_i, & for \quad i = 1,2 \quad and \; r &
\end{aligned}
$$

Hence

$$y = y_1 + y_2 = P_1 q_1 + P_2 q_2 = W(l_1 + l_2) \qquad (1.6)$$

and

$$1 = l_1 + l_2 + l_r \qquad (1.7)$$

This will serve to simplify our model, that seeks to find the equilibrium per capita production and consumption, as is revealed by the representative agent. The changing rate of the aging ratio is constant and is greater than 0.

$$\dot{l}_r / l_r = \theta_r \quad constant > 0 \qquad (1.8)$$

This implies that the labor force relative to the aging population is shrinking, although no assumptions are made about the growth rate of the population, N.

1.2 THE MODEL

The society is to choose q_1 and q_2 to maximize the social preference function (*)

$$\max_{q_1, q_2} U(q_1, q_2) \quad (*)$$

$$s.t. \; 1 = l_1 + l_2 + l_r$$

Literally, the society is to maximize the utility of per capita output, subject to the total labor constraint. This is equivalent to the maximization of the *social preference function*. Utility in the case of per capita consumption is measured as that of the representative agent, in that all individuals in the economy are assumed to rank preferences similarly. The form of the utility function is given further in this model.

Linear Production Transformation

Starting out with a simple case, we assume that production is a linear function of labor: $q_i = D_i l_i$ or

$$l_i = q_i/D_i, \quad i = 1, 2 \tag{1.9}$$

The per capita level of output per sector is simply the product of the fraction of the population in that sector (l_i) and the labor productivity (D_i). Productivity in this linear model is D_i and it represents average product, which is total output per total input (the marginal product equals average product in a linear production model). Consequently, at any time, labor is found by dividing productivity by output. We then can substitute this ratio into the initial labor constraint

$$1 - l_r = l_1 + l_2 \tag{1.10}$$

to arrive at the following

$$1 - l_r = q_1/D_1 + q_2/D_2 \tag{1.11}$$

Once the labor force constraint is transformed according to (11), the social preference constrained maximization from (*) is represented by the following Lagrangian:

$$L = U(q_1, q_2) + \lambda[(1 - l_r) - q_1/D_1 - q_2/D_2] \tag{1.12}$$

and solve for the first order condition given. We assume a concave increasing function for U in q_1 and q_2, in order to have an interior solution to the equations in (*)

$$\frac{\partial L}{\partial q_1} = U_1 - \lambda/D_1 = 0$$

$$\frac{\partial L}{\partial q_2} = U_2 - \lambda/D_2 = 0$$

$$\frac{\partial L}{\partial \lambda} = (1 - l_r) - q_1/D_1 - q_2/D_2 = 0$$

Then we get

$$U_2/U_1 = D_1/D_2 \tag{1.13}$$

Simplifying the variables we arrive at (13) that shows that the marginal rate of substitution of q_1 to q_2 in this two commodity, one input factor, consumption and linear production model is determined by the ratio of productivities of the two commodities. This represents a unique link between the marginal rate of substitution and the productivity measures based on the labor force constraint in the original objective function. At this time, we are deriving the static relationships in the model that is not to be confused with the dynamic nature of the model with respect to the time path of the simulations. Next, a zero profit condition assumes all revenue is paid to the factors of production, in this case, labor; hence,

$$
\begin{aligned}
P_i q_i &= W l_i \quad and \quad P_i(D_i.l_i) = W l_i \\
or\ D_i &= W/P_i \quad i = 1, 2
\end{aligned}
\tag{1.14}
$$

This is a result from (14) and it states that "real" wages or the purchasing power of wages in terms of prices, equals productivity. Then substituting W/P_i for D_i in (13) and cancelling the W term, we can extend the relationship of the marginal rate of substitution of q_1 to q_2 according to the following:

$$
\frac{U_2}{U_1} = \frac{D_1}{D_2} = \frac{P_2}{P_1}
\tag{1.15}
$$

As is common in most dual commodity models, the marginal rate of substitution equals the ratio of prices since prices move freely in these economies. Next, we find the relationship between the growth rate of prices and that of productivity.

$$
\frac{\dot{P_2}}{P_2} - \frac{\dot{P_1}}{P_1} = \gamma_1 - \gamma_2
\tag{1.16}
$$

Since the model addresses the relative prices of the health sector to the non-health sector by assuming the price in the non-health sector constant.

$$
\frac{\dot{P_1}}{P_1} = 0
$$

Thus, $\frac{\dot{P_2}}{P_2} = \gamma_1 - \gamma_2$. The specific form of the utility function can be given as

$$
U = \log\ q_1 + a.q_2^\alpha
\tag{1.17}
$$

where $0 < \alpha < 1$, so that utility is rising and is concave in both q_1 and q_2. Next, differentiating (17) and using (13) that gives the explicit form of the marginal rate of substitution as a function of the productivity ratios we get

$$
q_1 = \frac{D_1}{D_2} \frac{1}{a\alpha} q_2^{1-\alpha}
\tag{1.18}
$$

We then solve for the indifference curve. First we set $\alpha = 1/2$, and rearrange the utility function of (17). For a fixed level of utility $\overline{U}$, the indifference curves are as given:

$$q_1 = \exp(\overline{U} - aq_2^{\frac{1}{2}}) \tag{1.19}$$

where exp( ) represents the exponent function, the inverse of the natural log function.

When $q_2 = 0$, $q_1 = \exp(\overline{U})$

When $q_2 \to \infty$, $q_1 \to 0$

The graph of (19) yields the indifference curve of q_1 for q_2 (see figures 1 and 2). Note, this curve is negative-sloped and convex to the origin. This implies that at high levels of q_1 and low levels of q_2, the marginal utility is higher for q_2 and less for q_1. The marginal rate of substitution given by (18) for a fixed level of utility, $\overline{U}$, is measured as the slope of the line tangent to the indifference curve at that point, and this slope also equals the relative price ratios of the two commodities as is given in (15). Likewise, rearranging the labor force constraint in (11) yields the production transformation curve (PTC) in (20).

$$q_1 = -\frac{D_1}{D_2} \cdot q_2 + D_1(1 - l_r) \tag{1.20}$$

The slope of this curve like that of the indifference curve is negative but it is linear with respect to q_1 and q_2. This is consistent with homogeneity of labor that implies that at any level of output, the rate of transforming production away from one good to produce the other is constant and equals the ratio of productivity measures D_1/D_2, the slope of the line in (20), (see figures 1 and 2). The PTC is expanding over time since $D_i > 0$ and $\gamma_1 > \gamma_2$; that is, D_1 is growing at a faster rate than D_2, even though the relative share of the population in the non-health sector l_1 is shrinking. The marginal rate of transformation is also a *static* measurement, the slope of the line is linear even though D_1/D_2 is rising over time. Next, dividing (18) by q_2 yields the time path of the PTC given by (21). This time path is illustrated in figures 1 and 2, along with the indifference curves.

$$\frac{q_1}{q_2} = \frac{D_1}{D_2} \cdot (q_2^{-\frac{1}{2}}) \cdot \frac{2}{a} \tag{1.21}$$

Since a society consumes what is produced, the indifference curves are drawn tangent to the PTC and the equilibrium point of production/consumption is the point of tangency. The simulations hold the assumption that the production ratio, q_1/q_2 is constant over time. Note in the figures when this ratio is constant (figure 2) the time path, measured by the positively sloped line, is a straight line - the ratio rises by a constant rate over time. This relationship follows from assumption (8) concerning non-homothetic preferences. Recall in Japan's case q_1/q_2 is held at 22 and that in the U.S. is held at 12. When q_1/q_2 is not held constant, the time path is concave as is shown in figure 1. This concavity implies the law of diminishing returns in that less output, and hence less labor is used from the productivity-progressive sector while more labor is used for the production of the productivity-stagnant sector. See Appendix B for demand equations and elasticity of income measures.

General Production Transformation

The production function for each sector is now of the general form

$$q_i = f_i(l_i) \qquad for \; i = 1, 2 \qquad (1.22)$$

where $f_i' > 0$, $f_i'' < 0$, for $i= 1$, 2. The per capita output level in the economy is a concave, increasing function of labor. Output is rising in labor, but at a decreasing rate. Since $f_i' > 0$, we can assume that there exists the inverse function such that,

$$l_i = f_i^{-1}(q_i) = \varphi_i(q_i) \qquad for \; i = 1, 2 \qquad (1.23)$$

That is, the relative ratio of the population that work in each sector is a function of output in that sector such that $\varphi_i(f_i(l_i)) = l_i$. Therefore the following relationships hold:

$$\varphi_i' \;\; = \;\; \frac{1}{f_i'} > 0 \qquad (1.24)$$

$$\varphi_i'' \;\; = \;\; -\frac{f_i''}{f_i'^2} > 0 \qquad (1.25)$$

The fact that (24) is positive comes from the concavity of the original production function: since the numerator is negative, the denominator is positive, and the fraction is multiplied by (-1); the second derivative of the inverse function is in fact positive. The Lagrangian then becomes

$$L = U(q_1, q_2) + \lambda[(1 - l_r) - \varphi_1(q_1) - \varphi_2(q_2)] \qquad (1.26)$$

and solving for first order conditions yields the following:

$$\frac{U_2}{U_1} = \frac{\varphi_2'}{\varphi_1'} \qquad (1.27)$$

Since $P_i q_i = W l_i$ as was in the original model, and $l_i = \varphi_i(q_i)$, we can substitute $\varphi_i(q_i)$ for l_i so that $P_i q_i = W \cdot \varphi_i(q_i)$. Rearranging so that $\varphi_i(q_i) = \frac{P_i q_i}{W}$

simplifies the differentiation

$$\varphi_i' = \frac{P_i}{W} \tag{1.28}$$

Therefore following (10), we can substitute (26) into (25) to arrive at the following result:

$$\frac{U_2}{U_1} = \frac{\varphi_2'}{\varphi_1'} = \frac{P_2}{P_1} \tag{1.29}$$

In order to derive the production transformation curve, it is necessary to take the labor constraint equation, $1 - l_r = \varphi_1(q_1) + \varphi_2(q_2)$, and derive an equation of q_1 as a function of q_2, or

$$q_1 = \varphi_1^{-1}[(1 - l_r) - \varphi_2(q_2)]$$

Differentiating gives the following result:

$$q_1' = \frac{dq_1}{dq_2} = -\frac{\varphi_2'}{\varphi_1'} < 0 \tag{1.30}$$

$$q_1'' = -\frac{\varphi_1''(q_1')^2 + \varphi_2''}{\varphi_1'} < 0 \tag{1.31}$$

The PTC curve is negative and concave to the origin. This implies that the transformation of labor is not constant and there are diminishing returns to specialization in any output, unlike the linear case. If we set the production function as $q_i = (D_i l_i)^{\alpha_i}$, we can derive the inverse function for labor by

$$l_i = \varphi_i(q_i) = \frac{q_i^{\frac{1}{\alpha_i}}}{D_i} \tag{1.32}$$

where $0 < \alpha_i < 1$, for $i = 1, 2$. Differentiating (32) with respect to q_i we have the following :

$$\varphi_i'(q_i) = \frac{1}{\alpha_i} \cdot \frac{q_i^{\frac{1}{\alpha_i} - 1}}{D_i} \quad for \ i = 1, 2$$

Substituting (17) and (32) into (27) we get the corresponding time path

$$q_1 = \left(\frac{2}{a} \frac{D_1 \alpha_1}{D_2 \alpha_2} q_2^{1/\alpha_2 - 1/2}\right)^{\alpha_1} \tag{1.33}$$

which shows that q_1 is increasing in q_2. The indifference curve is the same as in (19). The production transformation curve then becomes

$$q_1^{\frac{1}{\alpha_1}} = -\frac{D_1}{D_2} q_2^{\frac{1}{\alpha_2}} + D_1(1 - l_r) \tag{1.34}$$

114

which is concave as discussed in (30) and (31). The time path, indifference curves and PTC of (22), (19) and (34) respectively, are shown in figure 3. The positively sloped, concave line is the time path; the dotted lines drawn convex to the origin are the indifference curves, the negatively sloped concave lines are the PTCs and the straight lines are the budget constraints: $y = P_1 q_1 + P_2 q_2$. The slope of this line, $(-P_2/P_1)$, equals the marginal rate of substitution of q_1 to q_2 at the point of tangency. This holds the same non-homothetic preferences as model 1, since the form of the utility function does not change.

1.3   SIMULATION EQUATIONS

Using model 1 and maintaining $Q_1/Q_2 = q_1/q_2 = $ constant, we have

$$\frac{\dot{q}_1}{q_1} = \frac{\dot{q}_2}{q_2} \tag{1.35}$$

In other words, the rate of growth in the per capita output is the same in both sectors. From $q_i = D_i l_i$, we can break down (35) with the following

$$\gamma_1 + \frac{\dot{l}_1}{l_1} = \gamma_2 + \frac{\dot{l}_2}{l_2} \tag{1.36}$$

where γ_i, is the growth rate of productivity in sector i. From (7), $1 = l_r + l_1 + l_2$, can be reduced to the following form:

$$\frac{l_2}{1 - l_r} = \left(1 - \frac{l_1}{1 - l_r}\right) \tag{1.37}$$

Differentiating (10) and dividing through by l_r gives us

$$-\frac{\dot{l}_r}{l_r} = \frac{\dot{l}_1}{l_r} + \frac{\dot{l}_2}{l_r} \tag{1.38}$$

Letting $\theta_r = \frac{\dot{l}_r}{l_r}$ we have

$$-\theta_r = \frac{\dot{l}_1}{l_r} + \frac{\dot{l}_2}{l_r}\frac{l_2}{l_2} \tag{1.39}$$

or

$$-\theta_r = \frac{\dot{l}_1}{l_r} + \frac{\dot{l}_2}{l_2}\frac{l_2}{l_r} \tag{1.40}$$

Now multiplying by $\frac{l_r}{l_2}$ we have

$$-\frac{\dot{l}_2}{l_2} = \theta_r\frac{l_r}{l_2} + \frac{\dot{l}_1}{l_2} \tag{1.41}$$

If we let $\gamma = \gamma_1 - \gamma_2$, from (36) we get the following relation:

$$\gamma = \frac{\dot{l_2}}{l_2} - \frac{\dot{l_1}}{l_1} \tag{1.42}$$

From (41) and (42), we have

$$\gamma + \frac{\dot{l_1}}{l_1} = -\theta_r \frac{l_r}{l_2} - \frac{\dot{l_1}}{l_2} \tag{1.43}$$

Rearranging, we have

$$\frac{\dot{l_1}}{l_1} + \frac{\dot{l_1}}{l_2} = -\theta_r \frac{l_r}{l_2} - \gamma \tag{1.44}$$

Isolating $\dot{l_1}$ from the LHS of (44), and rearranging we have

$$\dot{l_1}\left(\frac{l_2 + l_1}{l_1 l_2}\right) = -\theta_r \frac{l_r}{l_2} - \gamma \tag{1.45}$$

From (5), (45) becomes

$$\dot{l_1}\left(\frac{1 - l_r}{l_1 l_2}\right) = -\theta_r \frac{l_r}{l_2} - \gamma \tag{1.46}$$

We can derive the following form for l_1 remembering $l_2 = 1 - l_1 - l_r$:

$$\dot{l_1} + \left(\gamma + \frac{\theta_r l_r}{1 - l_r}\right) l_1 - \frac{\gamma}{1 - l_r} l_1^2 = 0 \tag{1.47}$$

Note this is a Bernoulli type differential equation,

$$\dot{l_1} + f(t).l_1 + g(t).l_1^2 = 0 \tag{1.48}$$

Solving it we get

$$l_1 = \frac{1 - l_r}{1 + \frac{l_{20}}{l_{10}}.e^{\gamma t}} \tag{1.49}$$

$$l_2 = \frac{1 - l_r}{1 + \frac{l_{10}}{l_{20}}.e^{-\gamma t}} \tag{1.50}$$

Where $f(t) = \gamma + \frac{\theta_r l_r}{1 - l_r}, g(t) = -\frac{\gamma}{1 - l_r}$ and l_{10} and l_{20} represent the initial conditions for both labor sets. For Japan $l_{10} = 82.00$ and $l_{20} = 6.00$. For the U.S. $l_{10} = 76.91$ and $l_{20} = 10.49$. We are particularly interested in P_2/P_1, and without loss of generality, we can assume that P_1 is held constant. Given the initial conditions and the values of parameters $(\gamma_1, \gamma_2, \theta_r)$, we can simulate the time series for $W, D_1, D_2, l_1, l_2, q_1, q_2, y_1, y_2, l_r$ and y. First, from the linear production function we have $q_i = D_i l_i$, where D_{i_0} is given and the growth rate of D_1 and D_2 is determined exogenously by γ_1 and γ_2. Next the wage rate is determined. As the model specifies, productivity gains in the non-health sector are met with equal wage increases that are passed on to the health sector. Therefore, wages grow at the same rate as productivity in the non-health sector. Finally, from the marginal rate of substitution derivation we were able to calculate the path of price movements in the health sector. After initial conditions for prices of both goods, the growth rate of prices evolves at a rate specified by $\gamma_1 - \gamma_2$. Note, this is not the same as health care inflation which measures the growth rate in the market value of goods, or $y_i = P_i q_i$. This then brings us to our final variables y, y_1 and y_2. The latter two are determined as in the previous sentence and y is merely the sum of the two market value of goods.

Appendix B
Proof that Income Elasticity is Greater than One

This appendix is primarily concerned with proving that income elasticity of
health is greater than one. This is consistent with the non-homotheticity of
preferences that is required to validate the assumption that q_1/q_2 is constant.
As time evolves and income rises, the economy is spending a larger percentage
of GDP on health services. Homothetic preferences require that as income rises,
the portion spent on both goods rises at an equal rate. This would mean that
y_1/y_2 would be constant, and clearly this is not possible if q_1/q_2 is constant
over time while P_2/P_1 is rising at the rate of $\gamma_1 - \gamma_2$. Hence, y_1/y_2 is decreasing
at a rate of $\gamma_1 - \gamma_2$.

Nevertheless, we derive the demand function for q_2 based on the original
utility function given by (15), $U = \log q_1 + a.q_2^\alpha$. Once we have the demand
function for q_2, we can derive the income elasticity measure which we show is
greater than one.

The objective function is as follows:

$$max_{q_1,q_2} U(q_1,q_2) = \log q_1 + a.q_2^\alpha$$
$$s.t.\ I = P_1.q_1 + P_2.q_2$$

where we hold $\alpha = \frac{1}{2}$.

Here the household is to maximize the utility of consumption, subject to
the standard budget constraint. This is equivalent to the maximization of the
household utility function. Utility in the case of consumption is measured
as that of the representative agent, in that all individuals in the economy are
assumed to rank preferences similarly.

$$L = \log q_1 + a.q_2^\alpha + \lambda(I - P_1.q_1 - P_2.q_2) \tag{B.1}$$

$$\frac{\partial L}{\partial q_1} = \frac{1}{q_1} - \lambda P_1 = 0 \tag{B.2}$$

$$\frac{\partial L}{\partial q_2} = \frac{a}{2}q_2^{-\frac{1}{2}} - \lambda P_2 = 0 \tag{B.3}$$

$$\frac{\partial L}{\partial \lambda} = I - P_1 q_1 - P_2 q_2 = 0 \tag{B.4}$$

Dividing (B.2) by (B.3) we have

$$\frac{2q_2^{\frac{1}{2}}}{aq_1} = \frac{P_1}{P_2} \tag{B.5}$$

or

$$q_1 = \frac{2q_2^{\frac{1}{2}}}{a}\frac{P_2}{P_1} \tag{B.6}$$

From (B.4) and (B.6) we have

$$I - P_1\left[\frac{2q_2^{\frac{1}{2}}}{a}\frac{P_2}{P_1}\right] - P_2q_2 = 0 \tag{B.7}$$

or

$$I - P_2\frac{2q_2^{\frac{1}{2}}}{a} - P_2q_2 = 0 \tag{B.8}$$

Simplifying, we have

$$\frac{I}{P_2} - \frac{2q_2^{\frac{1}{2}}}{a} - q_2 = 0 \tag{B.9}$$

Let $q_2^{\frac{1}{2}} = u$ so that $q_2 = u^2$, and rearranging (B.9) we get

$$u^2 + \frac{2}{a}u - \frac{I}{P_2} = 0 \tag{B.10}$$

Using the quadratic formula, we insert the coefficients in (B.10) to arrive at the following:

$$\frac{-\frac{2}{a} \pm \sqrt{\frac{4}{a^2} + 4\frac{I}{P_2}}}{2} = -\frac{1}{a} \pm \sqrt{\frac{1}{a^2} + \frac{I}{P_2}} = u \tag{B.11}$$

Since $q_2^{\frac{1}{2}} = u$ must be ≥ 0, it is safe to assume that we need only consider the positive root or

$$u = \sqrt{\frac{1}{a^2} + \frac{I}{P_2}} - \frac{1}{a}$$

or simplified

$$q_2 = \frac{2}{a^2} + \frac{I}{P_2} - \frac{2}{a}\sqrt{\frac{1}{a^2} + \frac{I}{P_2}} \tag{B.12}$$

which is the demand equation for health services. Differentiating with respect to income, we have

$$
\begin{aligned}
\frac{\partial q_2}{\partial I} &= \frac{1}{P_2} - \frac{2}{a} \cdot \frac{1}{2} \left(\frac{1}{a^2} + \frac{I}{P_2} \right)^{-\frac{1}{2}} \cdot \frac{1}{P_2} \\
&= \frac{1}{P_2} \left[1 - \frac{1}{a} \left(\frac{1}{a^2} + \frac{I}{P_2} \right)^{-\frac{1}{2}} \right] \\
&= \frac{1}{P_2} \left[1 - \frac{1}{a} \left(\frac{P_2 + Ia^2}{a^2 P_2} \right)^{-\frac{1}{2}} \right] \\
&= \frac{1}{P_2} \left[1 - \frac{1}{a} \left(\frac{a^2 P_2}{P_2 + Ia^2} \right)^{\frac{1}{2}} \right]
\end{aligned}
$$

or,

$$\frac{\partial q_2}{\partial I} = \frac{1}{P_2} \left[1 - \left(\frac{P_2}{P_2 + Ia^2} \right)^{\frac{1}{2}} \right] \tag{B.13}$$

If we invert (B.12), the demand equation, and multiply by I we get the following

$$\frac{I}{q_2} = \frac{a^2 P_2 I}{2P_2 + a^2 I - 2P_2((P_2 + Ia^2)/P_2)^{\frac{1}{2}}} \tag{B.14}$$

Multiplying (B.13) by (B.14) we get

$$\frac{\partial q_2}{\partial I} \frac{I}{q_2} = \frac{a^2 P_2 I}{2P_2 + a^2 I - 2P_2((P_2 + Ia^2)/P_2)^{\frac{1}{2}}} \cdot \tag{B.15}$$

$$\frac{1}{P_2} \left[1 - \left(\frac{P_2}{P_2 + Ia^2} \right)^{\frac{1}{2}} \right] \tag{B.16}$$

Let $v = \left(\frac{P_2}{P_2 + Ia^2} \right)^{\frac{1}{2}}$ and $2P_2 = c$, then (B.16) becomes

$$\frac{\partial q_2}{\partial I} \frac{I}{q_2} = \frac{a^2 I(1 - v)}{c + a^2 I - c\left(\frac{1}{v}\right)} \tag{B.17}$$

This exercise is to prove that the income elasticity of health services is greater than one, or that (B.17) ¿1, or simply

$$a^2 I(1-v) > a^2 I + c(1 - \frac{1}{v}) \tag{B.18}$$

or that

$$-Ia^2 v > c(1 - \frac{1}{v}) \tag{B.19}$$

$$I < \frac{c(1-v)}{a^2 v^2} \tag{B.20}$$

Substituting in for v where $v = \left(\frac{P_2}{P_2 + Ia^2}\right)^{\frac{1}{2}}$ in the denominator of (71) and for $c = 2P_2$, we arrive at

$$I < \frac{\left(P_2 + Ia^2\right) 2P_2(1-v)}{a^2 P_2} \tag{B.21}$$

which simplifies to

$$Ia^2 < 2\left(P_2 + Ia^2\right)(1-v) \tag{B.22}$$

Rearranging, we get the following:

$$Ia^2 + 2P_2 > 2v\left(P_2 + Ia^2\right) \tag{B.23}$$

Factoring out the final v we have

$$Ia^2 + 2P_2 > 2\left(\frac{P_2}{P_2 + Ia^2}\right)^{\frac{1}{2}}\left(P_2 + Ia^2\right) \tag{B.24}$$

Cancelling through gives us

$$Ia^2 + 2P_2 > 2P_2^{\frac{1}{2}}\left(P_2 + Ia^2\right)^{\frac{1}{2}} \tag{B.25}$$

Now, squaring the terms and simplifying we get,

$$\left(Ia^2\right)^2 + 4P_2^2 + 4P_2 Ia^2 > 4P_2\left(P_2 + Ia^2\right) \tag{B.26}$$

or

$$I^2 a^4 + 4P_2^2 + 4P_2 Ia^2 > 4P_2 + 4P_2 Ia^2 \tag{B.27}$$

which, after eliminating like terms, leaves us with simply proving that

$$I^2 a^4 \; > \; 0 \tag{B.28}$$
$$\forall \, a \; \neq \; 0$$

Thus, we have proved that the income elasticity of health services is greater than one.

BIBLIOGRAPHY

BIBLIOGRAPHY

Aaronson, M.K., D.C. Post, and P. Guastadisegni, 1993. "Dementia, Agitation, and Care in the Nursing Home." Journal of the American Geriatrics Society, Journal of the American Geriatrics Society, 41 (5), pp. 507-512.

Andersen, R. 1968. A Behavioral Model of Families' Use of Health Services. Chicago, Center for Health Administration Studies.

Andersen, R., and J. Newman. 1973. "Societal and Individual Determinants of Medical Care Utilization in the United States." Milbank Memorial Fund Quarterly, 5, pp. 95-124.

Arfken, C.L., H.W. Lach, S. McGee, S.J. Birge and J.P. Miller. "Visual Acuity, Visual Disabilities and Falling in the Elderly" Journal of Aging and Health, Vol. 6, No. 1, February 1994, pp. 38-50.

Avery, R., A. Speare Jr., and L. Lawton, 1989. "Social Support, Disability and Independent Living of Elderly Persons in the United States." Journal of Aging Studies, 3, pp. 279-293.

Badenhop, D.T., P.A. Cleary, S.F. Schaal, E.L. Fox, and B.L. Bartell, 1983. "Physiological Adjustment to Higher or Lower Intensity Exercise in Elders." Medicine and Science in Sports and Exercise, 15(6), pp. 496-502.

Bagley, S.P., and T.F. Williams, 1988. "Technology and Aging: The New Frontier." In G. Lesnoff-Caravaglia (Ed.), Aging in a Technological Society (pp. 19-25). New York, Human Science.

Baker, S. P. and A.H. Harvey, 1985. "Fall Injuries in the Elderly." Clinical Geriatric Medicine, 1, pp. 501-512.

Barrera, M., 1986. "Distinctions Between Social Support Concepts, Measures, and Models." American Journal of Community Psychology, 14, pp. 413-445.

Bass, D.M., and L.S. Noelker, 1987. "The Influence of Family Caregivers on Elder's Use of In-Home Services: An Expanded Conceptual Framework."Journal of Health and Social Behavior, 28, pp. 184-196.

Baum, B.J. (Ed.) 1992. "Oral and Dental Problems in the Elderly." Clinics in Geriatric Medicine. Philadelphia, W.B. Saunders.

Baumol, William J., "Private Affluence, Public Squalor", Economic Research Report #92-15, C.V. Starr Center for Applied Economics, New York University, April 1992.

Baumol, William J. 1986. "Productivity Growth, Convergence, and Welfare". American Economic Review 76 (December), pp. 1072-85.

Baumol, William J. (1985) "Productivity Policy and the Service Sector," in Robert Inman (ed.) Managing the Service Economy: Prospects and Problems, New York, Cambridge University Press.

Baumol, William J., Sue Anne Batey Blackman, and Edward N. Wolff. 1989. Productivity and American Leadership: The Long View. Cambridge, Mass. MIT Press.

Becker, Gary. 1962. "Investment in Human Capital: A Theoretical Analysis." Journal of Political Economy, Supplement, 70, pp. 9-44.

Becker, Gary. 1964. Human Capital: A Theoretical and Empirical Analysis with Special Reference to Education. New York: Columbia University Press

Beck, JD 1990. "The Epidemiology of Root Caries." Journal of Dental Research, 69, pp.1216-1221.

Binney, E.A., C.L. Estes, and S.R. Ingman. 1990. "Medicalization, Public Policy and the Elderly: Social Services in Jeopardy." Social Science Medicine 30:761-771.

Bishop, John. 1987. "The Recognition and Reward of Employee Performance." Journal of Labor Economics, 5, pp. S36-S56.

Blazer, D., D.C. Hughes, and K.L. George. 1987. "The Epidemiology of Depression in an Elderly Community Population." The Gerontologists, 27, pp. 281-287.

Blazer, D., and C.D. Williams. 1980. "Epidemiology of Dysphoria and Depression in an Elderly Population." American Journal of Psychiatry, 137, pp. 439-444.

Blinder, Alan S. (editor) (1990) Paying for Productivity: A Look at the Evidence. Washington, D.C., The Brookings Institution.

Bloom, B. 1982. Vital and Health Statistics, Current Estimates from the National Health Interview Survey, United States - 1981. [DHHS Publication No. PHS 82-1569, Series 10, No. 141]. Washington D.C., Government Printing Office.

Bloom B., H.C. Gift, and S.S. Jack. 1992. Dental Services and Oral Health: United States, 1989 [DHHS Publication No. PHS 93-1511, Series 10, No. 183]. Washington DC, U.S. Government Printing Office.

Borjas, George, J. 1983. "The Measurement of Race and Gender Wage Differentials: Evidence from the Federal Sector." Industrial and Labor Relations Review, 37, pp. 79-91.

Bortz, W. MM, 1980. "Effect of Exercise on Aging-Effect of Aging on Exercise." Journal of the American Geriatrics Society, 28, pp. 49-51.

Branch, L.G., A.A. Antczak, and W. B. Stason, 1986. "Toward Understanding the Use of Dental Services by the Elderly." Special Care in Dentistry, 6, pp. 38-41.

Brown, Richard. 1984. "Medicare and Medicaid: The Process, Value and Limits of Health Care Reform", in Meredith Minkler and Carroll Estes (editors), Readings in the Political Economy of Aging, New York, Baywood, pp. 117-143.

Buchele, Robert, and Mark Aldrich. 1985. "How Much Difference Would Comparable Worth Make?" Industrial Relations, 24, pp. 222-233.

Bucquet, D., and S. Curtis, 1986. "Socio-Demographic Variation in Perceived Illness and the Use of Primary Care: The Value of Community Survey Data for Primary Care Service Planning." Social Science and Medicine, 23, pp. 737-744.

Cape, Ronald T., Rodney M.Coe, and Isadore M. Rossman. 1984. Fundamentals of Geriatric Medicine. New York: Raven Press.

Caplan, A.L. 1986. "Economic and Social Issues." in A.S. Allen (ed.). New Options, New Dilemmas. Lexington, M.A., D.C. Heath.

Caspersen, C.J., G.M. Cristenson, and B.A. Pollard, 1986. "Status of the 1990 Fitness and Exercise Objectives: Evidence from N.H.I.S. 1985." Public Health Report, 101, pp. 587-592.

Center for Disease Control, 1989. "Surgeon General's Workshop on Health Promotion and Aging: Summary Recommendations of the Physical Fitness and Exercise Group." Journal of the American Medical Association, 262, pp. 2507-2510.

Chapleski, E.E. 1989. "Determinants of Knowledge of Services to the Elderly: Are Strong Ties Enabling or Inhibiting?" The Gerontologist 29:539-545.

Chrischilles, E.A., J.H. Lemke, R.B. Wallace, and G.A. Drube, 1990. "Prevalence and Characteristics of Multiple Analgesic Drug Use in an Elderly Study Group." Journal of the American Geriatric Society, 38, pp. 979-984.

Christensen, Laurits R. Dianne Cummings, and Dale W. Jorgenson. 1976. "Economic Growth, 1947-1973: An International Comparison," in John W. Kendrick and Beatrice Vaccara (editors), New Developments in Productivity Measurement, Studies in Income and Wealth, no. 44, National Bureau of Economic Research. New York: Columbia University Press.

Christensen, Laruits R. Dianne Cummings, and Dale W. Jorgenson. 1981. "Relative Productivity Levels, 1947-1973." European Economic Review 16 (may): pp. 61-94.

Conrad, K., and D. Jorgenson. 1985. "Sectoral Productivity Gaps Between the United States, Japan and Germany, 1960-1979." in Vereins fur Socialpolitik, Probleme und Perspektiven der Weltwirtschaftlichen Entwicklung, pp. 335-46. Berlin: Duncker and Humbolt.

Cook, A.J. and M.R. Thomas. "Pain and the Use of Health Services Among the Elderly," Journal of Aging and Health, Vol. 6, No. 2, May 1994, pp. 155-172

Coulton, C. and A.K. Frost. 1982. "Use of Social and Health Services by the Elderly." Journal of health and Social Behavior 23:330-339.

Czaja, S.J. 1988. "Safety and Security of the Elderly: Implications for Smart House Design." International Journal of Aging and Technology, 1, pp. 49-66.

Davis, Karen., Gerard F. Anderson, Diane Rowland, Earl P. Steinberg (1990) Health Care Cost Containment. Baltimore, The Johns Hopkins University Press.

Day, C.L. 1990. What Older Americans Think: Interest Groups and Aging Policy. Princeton: Princeton University Press.

Dean, Edwin, R., and Mark K. Sherwood. 1994. "Manufacturing Costs, Productivity, and Competitiveness, 1979-93." Monthly Labor Review, October, pp. 3-16.

Denison, Edward F., and William K. Chung. 1976. How Japan's Economy Grew so Fast, The Sources of Postwar Expansion. Washington, D.C.:Brookings.

Densen, Paul M., Sam Shapirp, and Marilyn Einhorn. 1959. "Concerning High and Low Utilizers of Service in a Medical Care Plan, and the Persistence of Utilization Levels Over a Three-Year Period." Milbank Memorial Fund Quarterly 37: 217-250.

Department of Health and Human Services. 1990. Health, United States, 1989. DHHS Publication 90-1232. Washington, D.C.: U.S. Government Printing Office.

deVries, H.A., 1970. "Physiological Effects of an Exercise Training Regimen Upon Men Aged 52-88." Journal of Gerontology, 25, pp. 325-336.

Diamond, P.A. 1965. "National Debt in a Neoclassical Growth Model." American Economic Review 55: 1126-1150.

Dickens, William T., and Kevin Lang. 1985. " A Test of Dual Labor Market Theory." American Economic Review, 5, pp. 792-805.

Dobelstein, A.W. and A.B. Johnson. 1985. Serving Older Adults: Policy, Programs, and Professional Activities. Englewood Cliffs, NJ: Prentice-Hall.

Dollar, David, and Edward No. Wolff. 1988. "Convergence of Industry Labor Productivity Among Advanced Economies". Review of Economics and Statistics 70 (November): pp. 549-58.

Dumas, Mark W. (1992) "Productivity in Industry and Government," Monthly Labor Review (June), pp. 48-57.

Ehrlich, I. and H. Chuma. 1990. "A Model of the Demand for Longevity and the Value of Life Extension." Journal of Political Economy 98: 761-782.

Ehrlich, I. and F.T. Lui. 1991. "Intergenerational Trade, Longevity,and Economic Growth." Journal of Political Economy 90: 1029-1059.

Eilers, M.L. 1989. "Older Adults and Computer Education: Not to Have Closed a Door." International Journal of Aging and Technology, 2, pp. 56-76.

Emery, Charles, F. 1994. "Effects of Age on Physiological and Psychological Functioning Among COPD Patients in an Exercise Program." Journal of Aging and Health, 6, February, pp. 3-16.

Englander, A. Steven, and Axel Mittelstadt. 1988. "Total Factor Productivity: Macroeconomic and Structural Aspects of the Slowdown." OECD Economic Studies 10 (Spring): pp. 8-56.

Estes, C.L. 1979. The Aging Enterprise. San Francisco, Jossey-Bass.

Estes, C.L. and Elizabeth A. Binney. 1989 "The Biomedicalization of Aging: Dangers and Dilemmas." The Gerontologist 29:587-596.

Exton-Smith, A.N. and P.W. Overstall, 1979. Geriatrics: Guidelines in Medicine. London, MTP Press Limited.

Ezell, M. and J.W. Gibson. 1989. "The Impact of Informal Social Networks on the Elderly's Need for Services." Journal of Gerontological Social Work 14:3-18.

Farmer, R.E. 1986. "Deficits and Cycles". Journal of Economic Theory 40, 77-88.

Fazzi, Robert A. (1994) Management Plus: Maximizing Productivity Through Motivation, Performance and Commitment. Burr Ridge, Illinois, Irwin Professional Publishing.

Felson, D. T., J.J. Anderson, M.T. Hannan, R.C. Milton, P.W. Wilson, and D.P. Kiel, 1989. "Impaired Vision and Hip Fracture: The Framingham Study." Journal of the American Geriatrics Society, 37, pp. 495-500.

Ferber, Mariane A., and Jane W. Loeb. 1974 "Professors, Performance and Rewards." Industrial Relations, 13, pp. 69-77.

Ferraro Kenneth F., and Thomas T.H. Wan. 1990. "Health Needs and Services for Older Adults: Evaluation Policies for an Aging Society" in Sidney M. Stahl, (ed.) The Legacy of Longevity: Health and Health Care in Late Life, Newbury Park, Sage Publications, pp. 235-269.

Ferrell, B.A., B.R. Ferrell, and D. Osterweil, 1990. "Pain in the Nursing Home." Journal of American Geriatrics Society, 38, pp. 409-414.

Fiatarone, M.A., E.C. Marks, N.D. Ryan, C.N. Meredith, L.A Lipsitz, and W. J. Evans, 1990. "High-intensity Strength in Nonagenarians: Effects on Skeletal Muscle." Journal of the American Medical Association 263 (22) pp. 3029-3034.

Fisher, Charles R., "Differences by Age Group in Health Spending," Health Care Financing Review 1, 1980, pp. 65-90.

Fitzgerald, J.T., S.P. Singleton, A.V. Neale, A.S. Prasad, and J.W. Hess, "Activity Levels, Fitness Status, Exercise Knowledge, and Exercise Beliefs Among Healthy, Older African-American and White Women." Journal of Aging and Health, Vol. 6, no. 3, August 1994, pp. 206-313

Fozard, J.L., E.J. Metter, and L.J. Brant. 1990. "Next Steps in Describing Aging and Disease in Longitudinal Studies." Journal of Gerontology, 45, pp. P116-P127.

Frank, Robert H. 1984. "Are Workers Paid their Marginal Product?" American Economic Review, 74, pp. 549-571.

Garber, Alan M. 1994. "Financing Health Care for Elderly Americans in the 1990s" in Yukio Noguchi and David A. Wise (eds.) Aging in the United States and Japan: Economic Trends. Chicago, The University of Chicago Press, pp. 175-194.

Gelfand, D.E. 1988. "The Aging Network: Programs and Services." New York, Springer.

Gilbert, G.H., R.P. Duncan, L.A. Crandall, and M.W. Heft, "Older Floridians' Attitudes Toward and Use of Dental Care." Journal of Aging and Health, Vol. 6, no. 1, February 1994, pp. 89-110.

Gilbert, G.H., and M.W. Heft, and R.P. Duncan, 1993. "Oral Signs, Symptoms, and Behaviors in Older Floridians." Journal of Public Health Dentistry, 53(3), pp. 151-157.

Gilbert, G.H., and M.W. Heft, 1992. "Periodontal Status of Older Floridians Attending Senior Activity Centers." Journal of Clinical Periodontology, 19, pp. 249-255.

Goldsteen, P.L., M.A. Counte, and K. Goldstein. "Examining the Relationship Between Health Locus of Control and the Use of Medical Care Services." Journal of Aging and Health, Vol. 6, no. 3, August 1994, pp. 314-335.

Gottlieb, B.H., and F. Wagner, 1991. "Stress and Social Support in Close Relationships." in J. Eckenrode (Ed.), The Social Context of Coping (pp. 165-188). New York, Plenum.

Greiner Mary, Christopher Kask, and Christopher Sparks. 1995. "Comperative Manufacturing Productivity and Unit Labor Costs." Monthly Labor Review, February, pp. 26-38.

Grisso, J.A., J.L. Kelsey, B.L. Strom, G.Y. Chiu, G. Maislin, L.A. O'Brien, S. Hoffman, F. Kaplan, and the Northeast Hip Fracture Study Group. 1991. "Risk Factors for Falls as a Cause of Hip Fracture in Women", New England Journal of Medicine, 324, pp. 1326-1331.

Grossman, M. 1972. The Demand for Health: A Theoretical and Empirical Investigation. New York. Columbia University Press (for NBER).

Hahm, W., and T. Bikson, 1989. "Retirees Using Email and Networked Computers." International Journal of Technology and Aging, 2, pp. 113-123.

Harkins, S.W., 1988. "Pain in the Elderly." in R. Dubner, G.F. Gebhart, and M.R. Bond (Eds.), Proceedings of the Vth World Congress on Pain (pp. 355-367). Amsterdam, Elsevier.

Harrington Meyer Madonna and Jill Quadagno. 1990. The Dilemma of Poverty-Based Long-Term Care" in Sidney M. Stahl (ed.) The Legacy of Longevity: Health and Health Care in Later Life, Newbury Park, Sage Publications, pp. 255-269.

Harris, S.S., C.J. Caspersen, G.H. DeFriese, and H.E. Estes, 1989. "Physical Activity Counseling for Healthy Adults as a Primary Preventive Intervention." Journal of the American Medical Association, 261 (24), pp. 3590-3598.

Hochschild, A.R., 1978. The Unexpected Community. Englewood Cliffs, NJ, Prentice-Hall.

Horan, Patrick M. 1978. "Is Status Attainment Research Atheoretical?" American Sociological Review, 43, pp. 534-541.

Hulten, Charles R. (ed.) 1990. Productivity Growth in Japan and the United States. Chicago: The University of Chicago Press.

Iglehart, John 1988. "Japan's Medical Care System." New England Journal of Medicine 319, pp. 807-812, 1166-1172.

Ikegami, Naoki, "Japanese Health Care: Low Cost Through Regulated Fees." Health Affairs, (10)8, 1991, pp. 87-109.

Irwin, M., and J. Pike, 1993. "Bereavement, Depressive Symptoms, and Immune Function." in M. S. Stroebe, S. Stroebe, and R. O. Hansson (Eds.), Handbook of Bereavement (pp. 160-171). New York, Cambridge University Press.

Ishimoto, T. 1989. "Japan's Medical Care Security System: Present Situation and New Policies", Hogaku Kiyo, no. 30, pp. 500-532.

Japan Productivity Center (1984) "Measuring Productivity: Trends and Comparisons from the First International Productivity Symposium." New York, UNIPUB, Asian edition co-published by the Asian Productivity Organization, Tokyo.

Jiyu-Minshuto. 1961. "Sosenkyo No Iei To Shinseisaku No Gaihyo" ("Meaning of the General Election and Comments on New Policy"), in Kokkai Nenkan 1961 (Diet yearbook 1961). Tokyo. Kokkai Nenkan Hakkokai.

Jorgenson, Dale W., and Zvi Griliches. 1967. "The Explanation of Productivity Change." Review of Economic Studies 34 (July): pp. 349-83.

Jorgenson, D.W., M. Kuroda, and M. Nishimizu. 1987. "Japan-U.S. Industry Level Productivity Comparison, 1960-1979." Journal of Japanese and International Economics 1 (1) pp. 1-30.

134

Kaiser M.A., H.J. Camp, and J. Gibbons. 1987. "Services for the Rural Elderly: A Developmental Model." Journal of Gerontological Social Work 11:25-45.

Kalleberg, Arne L., Michael Wallace, and Robert P. Althauser. 1981. "Economic Segmentation, Worker Power, and Income Inequality." American Journal of Sociology, 87, pp. 651-683.

Kanter, Rosabeth Moss. 1987. "From Status to Contribution: Some Organizational Implications of the Changing Basis for Pay." Personnel, 64, pp. 12-37.

Kart, C.S., E.K. Metress, and S.P. Metress, 1988. "Aging, Health and Society" (2nd ed.) (p. 43). Boston, Jones and Bartlett.

Katz, Laurence. 1986. "Efficiency Wages: A Partial Evaluation." National Bureau of Economic Research Macroeconomics Annual, pp. 235-276.

Kaufman, A.V. 1990. "Social Network Assessment: A Critical Component in Case Management for Functionally Dependent Older Persons." International Journal of Aging and Human Development 30:63-75.

Kendrick, John. 1961. "Productivity Trends in the United States." New York: National Bureau of Economic Research.

Kendrick, John. 1981. 'International Comparisons of Recent Productivity Trends." pp. 125-70, in William Fellner (ed.) Essays in Contemporary Economic Problems: Demand, Productivity, and Population. Washington, D.: American Enterprise Institute.

Kiyak, H.A., 1987. "An Explanatory Model of Older Person's Use of Dental Services: Implications for Health Policy." Medical Care, 25, pp. 936-952.

Kosloski, K, and R.J.V. Montgomery. 1994. "Investigating Patterns of Service Use by Families Providing Care for Dependent Elders." Journal of Aging and Health, 6, February, pp. 17-37.

Kovar, Mary Grace. 1986. "Expenditures for the Medical Care of Elderly People Living in the Community in 1980." Milbank Memorial Fund Quarterly 64:100-132.

Krause, Neal. 1990. "Illness Behavior in Later Life." in Robert H. Binstock and Linda K. George (Eds.), Handbook of Aging and the Social Sciences (3rd ed.). San Diego, CA: Academic Press.

Kunkel, Suzanne R., and Robert A. Applebaum, "Estimating the Prevalence of Long-Term Disability for an Aging Society", Journal of Gerontology: Social Sciences, Vol. 47, No. 5, 1992, pp. S253 S260.

La Buda, D.R. 1988, "Education, Leisure and Other Persons: Implications for Smart House Design." International Journal of Technology and Aging, 1, pp. 31-48.

Lair, J.T., and D.C. Lefkowitz, 1990. "Mental Health and Functional Status of Residents of Nursing and Personal Care Homes" (National Medical Expenditure Survey Research Findings 7). Rockville, MD, Agency for Health Care Policy and Research.

Laudenslage, M.L., and M.L. Reite, 1984. "Losses and Separations: Immunological Consequences and Health Implications." in P. Shaver (Ed.), Review of Personality and Social Psychology (pp. 285-312). Beverly Hills, CA., Sage.

Leake, J. 1990. "An Index of Chewing Ability." Journal of Public Health Dentistry, 50, pp. 242-267.

Leu, R.R., "The Public-Private Mix and International Health Care Costs," in Cylyer, A.J., and Jonsson B., eds. Public and Private Health Services: Complementarities and Conflicts, Basil Blackwell, Oxford, England, 1986.

Levit, K.R., H.C. Lazenby, C.A. Cowan, and S.W. Letsch, 1991. "National Health Expenditures." Health Care Financing Review, 13, pp. 29-54.

Levy, Jesse, et al., "Impact of the Medical Fee Schedule on Payments to Physicians." Journal of the American Medical Association, 264, 1990, pp. 717-722.

Liu Korbin, Pamela Doty, and Kenneth Manton. 1990. "Medicaid Spenddown in Nursing Homes." The Gerontologist 30 (1), pp. 7-15.

Locker, D., and M. Grushka, 1987, "The Impact of Dental and Facial Pain." Journal of Dental Research, 66, pp. 1414-1417.

136

Lord, S.R., R.D. Clark, and I.W. Webster, 1991. "Postural Stability and Associated Physiological Factors in a Population of Aged Persons." Journal of Gerontology, 46, pp. M69-M76.

Mahler, D.A., R.A. Rosiello, and J. Loke. 1986. "The Aging Lung." Geriatric Clinics of North America, 2, pp. 215-225.

Manton, K.G., L. Corder, and E. Stallard, 1993. "Changes in the Use of Personal Assistance and Special Equipment from 1982 to 1989: Results from the 1982 and 1989 NLTCS." The Gerontologists, 33, pp. 168-176.

McCall, Nelda and Hoi S. Wai. 1983. "Analysis of the Use of Medical Services by the Continuously Enrolled Aged." Medical Care 21:567-585.

McFarland, Bentson H., Donald K. Freeborn, John P. Mullooly, and Clyde E. Pope. 1985. "Utilization Patterns Among Long-term Enrollees in a Prepaid Group Practice Health Maintenance Organization." Medical Care 23:1221-1233.

McGuire, Thomas G., and Mark Pauly, "Physician Response to Fee Changes with Multiple Payers." Journal of Health Economics, 10, 1991.

McSweeny, A.J., I. Grant, R.K. Heaton, K.M. Adams, and R.M. Timms. 1982. "Life Quality of Patients with Chronic Obstructive Pulmonary Disease." Archives of Internal Medicine, 142, pp. 473-478.

Medoff, James L., and Katherine G. Abraham. 1980. "Experience, Performance, and Earnings." Quarterly Journal of Economics, 95, pp. 703-736.

Mincer. Jacob. 1970. "The Distribution of Labor Incomes: A Survey." Journal of Economic Literature, 8, pp. 1-26.

Mobily, P.R., K.A. Herr, M.K. Clark, and R. B. Wallace. "An Epidemiologic Analysis of Pain in the Elderly." Journal of Aging and Health, Vol. 6, no. 2, May 1994, pp. 139-154.

Mossey, Jana M., Betty Havens, and Fredric D. Wolinsky. 1989. "The Consistency of Formal Health Care Utilization: Physician and Hospital Utilization." in Marcia G. Ory and Kathleen Bond (eds.), Aging and Health Care: Social Science and Policy Perspectives. New York, Routledge.

Mossey, Jana and Evelyn Shapiro, "Physician Use by the Elderly Over an Eight-Year Period." American Journal of Public Health, 75, 1985, pp. 133-34.

Mutran, Elizabeth and Kenneth F. Ferraro, "Medical Need and Use of Services Among Older Men and Women." Journal of Gerontology: Social Sciences 43, 1988, S167-71.

Nadiri, M. Ishaq. 1970. "Some Approaches to the Theory and Measurement of Total Factor Productivity: A Survey." Journal of Economic Literature 8 (December): pp. 1137-77.

National Center for Health Statistics, 1960. "Dental Care: Interval and Frequency of Visits, United States, July, 1957-June, 1959." [Health Statistics from the National Health Interview Survey, Series B, No. 14, Public Health Service Publication No. 584-B14]. Washington, D.C., U.S. Government Printing Office.

National Center for Health Statistics, 1977. "Vital and Health Statistics, Current Estimates from the National Health Interview Survey." United States - 1975. [DHEW Publication No. HRA 77-1543, Series 10, No. 115]. Washington, D.C., U.S. Government Printing Office.

National Center for Health Statistics, "Health Statistics on Older Persons." United States, 1986. Vital and Health Statistics 3 (25), 1987.

Nevitt, M.C., S.R. Cummings, and E.S. Hudes, 1991. "Risk Factors for Injurious Falls: A Prospective Study." Journal of Gerontology, 46, pp. M164-M170.

Nishimizu, Mieko, and Charles R. Hulten. 1978. "The Sources of Japanese Economic Growth, 1955-71." Review of Economics and Statistics 60 (August): pp. 351-61.

Norsworthy, J.R. and D.H. Malmquist. 1983. "Input Mesurement and Productivity Growth in Japan and U.S. Manufacturing." American Economic Review 73 (6): pp. 947-67.

Ogura Seiritsu. 1994. The Cost of Aging: Public Finance Perspectives for Japan', in Yukio Noguchi and David A. Wise (eds.) Aging in the United States and Japan: Economic Trends. Chicago, The University of Chicago Press, pp. 139-173.

Okun, M.A., W.A. Stock, M.J. Haring, and R. Witter. 1984. "Health and Subjective Well-being: A Meta-analysis." International Journal of Aging and Human Development, 19, pp. 111-132.

Older American Act of 1965. U.S. Code 42 Section 3001.

Olson, L.K. 1982. The Political Economy of Aging. New York, Columbia University Press.

Organization for Economic Cooperation and Development (OECD), Health Care Systems in Transition: The Search for Efficiency, Paris 1990.

Osterweis, M., F.Solomon, and M. Green, (Eds.), 1984. Bereavement: Reactions, Consequences, and Care. Washington, D.C., National Academy of Science.

Over, R. 1966. "Possible Visual Factor in Fall by Old People." The Gerontologist, 6, pp. 212-214.

Owsley, C. and M.E. Sloane, 990. "Vision and Aging", in F. Boller and J. Grafman (Eds.), Handbook of Newropsychology: Volume IV (pp. 229-249). Amsterdam: Elsevier Science Publisher.

Parkin, David, Alistair McGuire, and Brian Yule, "Aggregate Health Care Expenditures and National Income: Is Health Care a Luxury Good?" Journal of Health Economics, 6, 1987, pp. 109-128.

Perkins, H.W., and L. B. Harris, 1990. "Familial Bereavement and Health in Adult Life Course Perspective." Journal of Marriage and the Family, 52(1), pp. 233-241.

Physician payment Review Commission "Price Controls for Medical Services and the Medical Needs of the Nation's Elderly." Paper Commissioned by the American Medical Association and presented to the Physician Payment Review Commission, March 18, 1988.

Prigatano, G.P., O. Parsons, E. Wright, D.C. Levin, and G. Hawryluk. 1983. "Neuropsychological Test performance in Mild Hypoxemic Patients with Chronic Obstructive Pulmonary Disease." Journal of Consulting and Clinical Psychology, 51, pp. 108-116.

The Public Interest "Containing Medical Costs: Why Price Controls Won't Work."
   The Public Interest, No. 93, Fall 1988, pp. 37-53.

Reavon, P.D., E. Barrett-Conner, and S. Edelstein, 1991. "Relation Between Lei-
   sure-Time Physical Activity and Blood Pressure in Older Women." Circulation,
   83, pp. 559-565.

Reichlin, P. 1986 "Equilibrium Cycles in an Overlapping Generations Economy
   with Production." Journal of Economic Theory 40:89-102.

Reisine, S.T., and J. Miller, 1985. "A Longitudinal Study of Work Loss Related to
   Dental Diseases." Social Science and Medicine, 21, pp. 1309-1314.

Rice, D.P., E.J. MacKenzie, and Associates, 1989. "Cost of Injury in the United
   States: A Report to Congress. San Francisco." Institute for Health and Aging,
   University of California and Injury Prevention Center, John Hopkins University.

Rice, Dorothy P. and Jacob J. Feldman. 1981. "Living Longer in the United States:
   Demographic Changes and Health Needs of the Elderly." Milbank Memorial
   Fund Quarterly 61:362-396.

Robertson, A. 1990. "The Politics of Alzheimer's Disease: A Case Study in
   Apocalyptic Demography." International Journal of Health Services 20:429-
   442.

Rodin, J., 1986. "Aging and Health: Effects of the Sense of Control." Science, 233,
   pp. 1271-1276.

Roos, Noralou P. Evelyn Shapiro, and Robert Tate. 1989. "Does a Small Minority
   of Elderly Account for a Majority of Health Care Expenditures? A Sixteen-
   Year Perspective." Milbank Memorial Fund Quarterly 67:347-369. Rosen-
   bloom, C.A., and F.J. Whittington, 1993. "The Effects of Bereavement on Eat-
   ing Behaviors and Nutrient Intakes in Elderly Widowed Persons." Journal of
   Gerontology: Social Sciences, 48, pp. S223-S229.

Ross, Noralou P., Evelyn Shapiro, and Leslie L. Roos, Jr., "Aging and the Demand
   for Health Services: Which Aged and Whose Demand?", The Gerontologist 24,
   1984, pp. 31-36.

Roy, R., and M.R. Thomas, 1986. "Elderly Persons With and Without Pain: A Comparative Study," Clinical Journal of Pain, 3, pp. 102-106.

Samuelson, P.A. 1958. "An Exact Consumption-Loan Model of Interest with or Without the Social Contrivance of Money." Journal of Political Economy 66: 467-482.

Sanders, C.M., 1993. "Risk Factors in Bereavement Outcome." M.S. Stroebe, W. Stroebe, and R.O. Hansson (Eds.), Handbook of Bereavement (pp. 255-267). New York, Cambridge University Press.

Scharlach, A.E., M.C. Runkle, L.T. Midanik, and K. Soghikian. "Health Conditions and Service Utilization of Adults with Elder Care Responsibilities." Journal of Aging and Health, vol. 6, no. 3, August 1994, pp. 336-352.

Schieber, George J. and Jean-Pierre Poullier, "International Health Care Expenditure Trends." Health Affairs, 8:3, Fall 1989, pp. 169-177.

Schleifer, S.J., S.E. Keller, M. Camerino, J.C. Thornton, and M. Stein, 1983. "Suppression of Lymphocyte Stimulations Following Bereavement." Journal of the American Medical Association, 250, pp. 347-377.

Schoenburn, C.A., 1986. "Health Habits of U.S. Adults 1985: The 'Alemeda 7' Revisited." Public Health Report, 101, pp. 571-580.

Semyonov, Moshe. 1988. "Bi-ethnic Labor Markets, Mono-Ethnic Labor Markets, and Socioeconomic Inequality." American Sociological Review, 53, pp. 256-266.

Semyonov, Moshe, and Vered Kraus. 1983. "Gender, Ethnicity, and Income Inequality: The Israel Experience." International Journal of Comparative Sociology, 24, pp. 258-272.

Senate Committee on Aging. 1988. "Developments in Aging, 1987: Volume III, the Long Term Care Challenge", February 29.

Shapira, David. 1984 " Wage Differentials Among Black, Hispanic, and White Young Men." Industrial and Labor Relations Review, 37, pp. 570-581.

Sharpe, P.A., and C.M. Connell, 1992. "Exercise Beliefs and Behaviors Among Older Employees: A Health Promotion Trial." The Gerontologist, 32, pp. 444-449.

Sibson, Robert E. (1994) Maximizing Employee Productivity: A Manager's Guide. New York, Amsterdam, American Management Association.

Silverstein, M., and V.L. Bengston, 1991. "Do Close Parent-Child Relations Reduce the Mortality Risk of Older Parents?" Journal of Health and Social Behavior, 32, pp. 382-395.

Slade, G.D., and A.J. Spencer, 1991. "The Development and Testing of the Oral Health Impact Profile." Journal of Dental Research, 70, pp. 382.

Smith, V.K. and R. Eggelston. 1989. "Long-Term Care: The Medical Versus the Social Model." Public Welfare 47:26-29.

Steslicke, William E. 1991. "Medical Care Security and the 'Vitality of the Private Sector' in Japan" in Christa Altenstetter and Stuart C. Haywood (eds.) Comparative Health Policy and the new Right: From Rhetoric to Reality. New York. St. Martin's press. pp. 247-282.

Steslicke, W.E. and R. Kimura. 1985. "Medical Technology for the Elderly in Japan." International Journal of Technology Assessment in Health Care no. 1, pp. 27-39.

Stoller, E.P., and L.L. Earl, 1983. "Help With Activities of Everyday Life: Sources of Support for the Noninstitutionalized Elderly." The Gerontologist, 23, pp. 64-70.

Stroebe, M.S., R.O. Hansson, and W. Stroebe, 1993. "Contemporary Themes and Controversies in Bereavement Research." In M.S. Stroebe, W. Stroebe, and R.O. Hansson (Eds.), Handbook of Bereavement (pp. 457-475). New York, Cambridge University Press.

Stroller, E.P., and L.E. Forster. "The Impact of Symptom Interpretation on Physician Utilization." Journal of Aging and Health, Vol. 6, no. 4, November 1994, pp. 507-534

Tolbert, Charles M., II , Patrick Horan, and E.M. Beck. 1980. "The Structure of Economic Segmentation: A Dual Economy Approach." American Journal of Sociology, 85, pp. 1095-1116.

Treiman, Donald J., and Kermit Terrell. 1975 "Sex and the Process of Status Attainment: A Comparison of Working Women and Men." American Sociological Review 40, pp. 174-200.

Trick, G.L., and S.E. Silverman, 1991. "Visual Sensitivity to Motion: Age-Related Changes and Deficits in Senile Dementia of the Alzheimer Type." Neurology, 41, pp. 1437-1440.

Tzankoff, S.P., S. Robinson, F.S. Pyke, and C.A. Brown, 1972. "Physiological Adjustment to Work in Older Men as As Affected by Physical Training." Journal of Applied Physiology, 33, pp. 346-350.

Umberson, D., 1987. "Family Status and Health Behaviors: Social Control as a Dimension of Social Integration." Journal of Health and Social Behavior, 28, pp. 306-318.

U.S. Bureau of the Census. 1984. Projections of the Population of the U.S. by Age, Sex, and Race; 1983-2080. Current Population Reports, ser. P-25, no. 952. Washington, D.C., Government Printing Office.

U.S. Department of Labor, Bureau of Labor Statistics. 1983. Trends in Multifactor Productivity, 1948-81. Bulletin no. 2178. Washington, D.C.: Government Printing Office (September).

U.S. Select Committee on Aging, H.R., Less Profit, Less Care? Reassessing the Impact of Medicare and Medicaid Cuts on Patients, Vol. 1, 2., Government Printing Office, Washington, D.C. 1988.

U.S. Senate Special Committee on Aging. 1986. Aging America: Trends and Projections (1985-86 ed.). Washington, D.C., Government Printing Office.

U.S. Senate Committee on Aging, Developments in Aging, 1987: Volume III, The Long Term Care Challenge, February 29, 1988.

U.S. Senate Special Committee on Aging, America in Transition: An Aging Society, Government Printing Office, Washington, D.C. 1985.

Verms, S.B. 1991. "Vision Ignored in Study of Falls." [Letter to the Editor]. The Gerontologist, 31, p. 417.

Waldo Daniell, et al. 1989. "Health Expenditures by Age Group: 1977 and 1987." Health Care Financing Review, 10:4, Summer, pp. 111-120.

Walker, Susan N. "Promoting healthy Aging" in Ferraro, K.F., Editor, Gerontology: Perspectives and Issues, Springer, New York 1990.

Wallston, K.A., S. Maides, and B.S. Wallston, 1976. "Health-Related Information Seeking as a Function of Health-related Locus of Control and Health Value." Journal of Research in Personality, 10, pp. 215-222.

Wan, Thomas T.H. 1989. "The Behavioral Model of Health Care Utilization by Older People." in Marcia Ory and Kathleen Bond (Eds.), Aging and Health Care. New York, Routledge.

Weir, R. F. 1989. "Abating Treatment with Critically Ill Patients: Ethical and Legal Limits to the Medical Prolongation of Life." New York, Oxford University Press.

Wolinsky, Fredric D. 1990. "Health and Health Behavior Among Elderly Americans: An Age-Stratification Perspective." New York: Springer.

Wolinsky, Fredric D. and Connie L. Arnold. 1988. "A Different Perspective on Health and health Services Utilization." Annual Review of Gerontology and Geriatrics 8:71-101.

Wolinsky, Fredric D. and Robert J. Johnson. 1991. "The Use of Health Services by Older Adults." Journal of Gerontology: Social Sciences 46:S345-S357.

Wolinsky, F. 1990. Health and Health Behavior Among Elderly Americans: An Age-Stratification Perspective." New York, Springer.

Wolinsky, Fredric, Ray Mosely, and Rodney Coe, "A Cohort Analysis of the Use of Health Services by Elderly Americans." Journal of Health and Social Behavior, 27, 1986, pp. 209-19

Yashiro Naohiro. 1995. "Japan's Economy in the Year 2020: The Complementary Relationship Between the Aging of the Population and Internationalization of the Economy." Japan Center for Economic Research Report, Vol. 7, No. 3, March 1995, pp. 3-6

Yellen, Janet. 1984. "Efficiency Wage Models of Unemployment." American Economic Review Papers and Proceedings, (May), pp. 200-205.

Yeo, G. and L. McGann. 1986. "Utilization by Family Physicians of Support Services for Elderly Patients." The Journal of Family Practice 22"431-434.

Yogev, Abraham, and Rina Shapira. 1987. "Ethnicity, Meritocracy, and Credentialism in Israel: Elaborating the Credential Society Thesis." Research in Social Stratification and Mobility, 6, pp. 187-212.

Zedlewski, S.R., R.O. Barnes, M.R. Burt, T.D. McBride, and J.A. Meyer (1990). "The Needs of the Elderly in the 21st Century." Washington, D.C., Urban Institute Press.

Zimmer, Z., and N.L. Chappcll. "Mobility Restriction and the Use of Devices Among Seniors." Journal of Aging and Health, Vol. 6, no. 2, May 1994, pp. 185-208

INDEX